Reminiscences of John Adye Curran

John Adye Curran, Longmans, Green and Co., Edward Arnold

BIBLIOLIFE

REMINISCENCES OF
JOHN ADYE CURRAN

K.C.

LATE COUNTY COURT JUDGE AND CHAIRMAN
OF QUARTER SESSIONS

WITH PORTRAIT

NEW YORK
LONGMANS, GREEN & CO.
LONDON: EDWARD ARNOLD
1915

TO

ROSE

FOR OVER HALF A CENTURY

MY DEAR WIFE AND HELPMATE

𝕴 𝕯𝖊𝖉𝖎𝖈𝖆𝖙𝖊 𝖙𝖍𝖊𝖘𝖊 𝕵𝖔𝖙𝖙𝖎𝖓𝖌𝖘

PREFACE

A NOT unfrequent fashion with compilers of " Reminiscences " is to make their preludial bow with an apology or form of justification. In sending forth this volume I shall not take the trouble to apologize or to justify. In the great adventure of life it is given to some men to play a little part in one or more of these incidents which mark the progress of a nation. The ever-increasing sum of such incidents when placed by the historian in the right perspective is called history. For me the investigation into the aims and deeds of the hideous Invincible Conspiracy which culminated in the assassination of Lord Frederick Cavendish and Mr. Thomas Henry Burke, on May 6, 1882, has been such an event. In the thirty-two years which have elapsed, not one of the many who have endeavoured to tell that bloody story has succeeded either in a correct statement of the facts or the proper appraisement of the motives of the assassins.

Having regard to my judicial position, I have been hitherto unable to contradict the various false and incorrect accounts of what took place at the investigation held by me.   And so it has occurred to me that the " Head Inquisitor of Dublin Castle," as I have been called, should employ his leisure hours in writing a true account of that dark chapter in Ireland's history.   Such a gruesome tale requires relief.   In Ireland, to an even greater extent than in the sister isle, the profession of the law brings its votaries into close touch with men and affairs.   During a busy and, thank God, a long and happy life, I have met many of the outstanding personalities of Irish history, and I have endeavoured "to save and recover from the deluge of time" some stories and recollections of those men who have passed into the shadows, and of the little customs and institutions—for instance, the Old Home Circuit—which with them have also faded.

J. A. C.

September, 1915.

CONTENTS

ix

CONTENTS

REMINISCENCES OF
JOHN ADYE CURRAN, K.C.

CHAPTER I

BOYHOOD AND COLLEGE DAYS

I TRUST it will not be ascribed either to presumption or vanity in me when I say that I hope and expect the contents of the following pages—some personal, some political, and covering, as they do, a period of over three-quarters of a century—may prove of interest to the public in general and to my professional brethren in particular.

In writing these reminiscences it is only right that I should in the first instance refer to my father, the late John Adye Curran, a barrister well known in Dublin and on the Home Circuit, to whom I owe so much. Having previously graduated in Trinity College, Dublin, he was called to the Bar in the year 1833. His call had been delayed by the Benchers for some time in consequence of a speech made by him during the Tithe Agitation, with the result that he had been tried at the Commission

1

in Green Street Court-house, and sentenced to a term of six months' imprisonment. He informed me that it was the late Baron Green who finally induced the Benchers to waive their objection.

My father was a very able criminal lawyer and defender of prisoners. He was engaged in all the cases of any note on circuit and in Dublin, from the date of his call in 1833 to that of his death in 1868. He was married in the year 1834. My mother was an English lady named Dolman, whose family came from Pocklington, Yorkshire. Her ancestors founded the Grammar School which still exists in that town, and is known as the " Dolman Grammar School." Her brother was the late Dr. John Thomas Dolman, formerly of York and afterwards of Souldern Aynho, Oxfordshire.

At the time of my birth in the year 1837, my father lived in what was then 68, Marlborough Street, but the number of the house has since been altered. That street was at that period the abode of young professional men, and my father bought the interest in the house from Dr. McKeever, who migrated to Cavendish Row. At the age of seven I went with my father to Paris to meet my mother, who had been wintering in the south of France, where she had gone for the benefit of her health. On our return we moved to 22, Lower Dominick Street, which street was then inhabited principally by leading barristers and solicitors.

Recollections of even very distinguished men

before the age of seven—the age under which even the law imputes impotency of crime—are rarely of interest, and are too often open to the suspicion that the recollection is of the nurse, and not the child. There are two events, however, of early childhood that are still green. As a prelude to a volume of stories of a stormy career, it is perhaps fitting that the great storm of 1839 should be the first milestone in my memory. During that terrible night a stack of chimneys was blown down through the skylight of our house, and I remember being brought for safety to pass the remainder of the night in the kitchen.

Till the day of his death I was the constant companion of my father, and one day, whilst still very young, I was walking with him in Great Britain Street, when we met a big man, enveloped in a cloak. He spoke to my father for a few moments and shook hands with me. When he had passed on, my father told me it was Daniel O'Connell. The momentary contact of a mere child with the great could not have the slightest degree of influence, but, nevertheless, while those who have even seen the great Liberator are growing fewer and fewer, it is a satisfaction to have held the hand of one who won so much for his country.

My first schooling was under a Dr. O'Toole, in York Street, Kingstown, but only for a short time. I then went to the Jesuits in Belvidere College, and afterwards for nearly four years to a school in Boulogne, at the head of which was Monseigneur Haffreingue. It was through the exertions of this clergyman that the splendid church and tower of Notre Dame in that town was built. I returned home in the year 1853, and was sent to the school in Harcourt Street, kept by Dr. James Quin, afterwards Bishop of Queensland, in Australia. I had there for masters, Dr. Matthew Quin, afterwards Bishop of Maitland, in Australia; Dr. Flannery, late Bishop of Killaloe; and the Most Rev. Dr. Robert Dunne, present Archbishop of Brisbane; and also the late Bishop Murray. As schoolfellows I had Sir Dennis Fitzpatrick, afterwards Lieut.-Governor of Punjab, General Sir Willian Butler, and his brother Thomas, who in after years, as resident magistrate, assisted me in my duties in the county Kerry. I had also for my schoolmates Dr. More Madden, Canon Conlan, and the Venerable Archdeacon Fricker, P.P., and many others distinguished in various walks of life. Some of them are still with us, but most have gone over to the great majority. In later years Dr. Walsh, Catholic Archbishop of Dublin, and my friend the Right Rev. Monsignor Fitzpatrick, P.P., V.G., brother of Sir Dennis Fitzpatrick, were also students in the same school.

I passed in the year 1855 from Dr. Quin's school to Trinity College. My father preferred I should go to that ancient seat of learning than to the

Catholic University, which had just been opened, as I thereby saved two years in my course for the Bar.· The Rev. Hewitt R. Poole was my tutor, a most kindly gentleman and cultured scholar. I remember one day chatting with him just inside the College gates, when two students passed. "Do you see those two young men?" he said to me. "Mark my words, they will yet make their mark in Irish history." He was prophetic: one was Edward Gibson, afterwards Lord Ashbourne, a Cabinet Minister and Lord Chancellor; the other was Gerald Fitzgibbon, afterwards Lord Justice of Appeal.

I never saw my tutor after I had left college until one day shortly before his death, when I was sitting opposite to him in a tram-car. I spoke to him; he, of course, did not recognize me until I mentioned my name, when he seemed delighted to meet me. He said he had watched my career from the day I left his care. It was a great pleasure to me that I was afterwards in a position to appoint his son, Mr. H. R. Poole, a rising barrister, as my counsel in the Midland Counties. I am sorry it was not a more lucrative post.

At such a great length of time I cannot remember many details of my college life. I suppose I was a very average student. It has been said that in those times a Catholic student in Trinity College ran the risk of losing his faith. Such was not my experience, as during my four years' stay in that University not a word was ever spoken to me by the College authorities on the subject. But, from my point of view as a Catholic, I consider it very wrong that I was not taught my religion by a professor of my faith.

A boy of sixteen to eighteen years is just of the age that requires to be looked after and kept up to the practices of his religion, especially if he is not resident with his family. Catholics in Trinity College never heard their religion or its practices mentioned, while all my brother Protestant students were much better looked after in this respect, and were awarded valuable premiums for efficiency in their religious studies. Nowadays much less interest is taken in the religious side of the education of the great Universities, so, with a sigh for these other *tempora et mores*, I shall pass on to the story of a mark on the top of my head, which has been my constant companion since college days.

On the occasion of the second entry of the Earl of Eglinton as Lord-Lieutenant of Ireland, in the year 1858, the students of Trinity College had to be confined within the space bounded by the front railings. Outside the place was guarded by a number of Metropolitan Police and mounted men. The students who lined the inside of the railings caused much confusion among the men and horses by bombarding them with crackers, which, when exploding, rendered the horses quite unmanageable.

Matters became so bad that the gates had to be flung open and the police ordered to charge with their batons.

I was standing some distance inside the gate looking on, when I felt myself taken possession of by three or four constables. They happened to know me from seeing me with my father, and they put me outside the gate and told me to go home. I took their advice, and was proceeding along the outside of the rails, when, glancing in, I saw a young friend knocked down and left lying on the ground. Intending to go to his assistance, I climbed back over the rails, and was going across to him, when I received a blow on the top of my head from a baton. I thought nothing of it, and went to help my friend. At this time the students had nearly all been driven by the police within the inner gate, and I was enabled to get quietly out, much discomfited and crestfallen. On my way home I discovered that my head and neck were all covered with blood, as a result of the stroke of the baton. I still bear the mark on the top of my head, but fortunately a good crop of hair conceals it. The late Dr. Nedley made the occasion of the charge and subsequent inquiry remarkable in a well-known song composed by him.

CHAPTER II

EARLY DAYS AT THE BAR—HINTS TO YOUNG BARRISTERS

Long before I became a law student I was a frequenter of the Law Courts with my father, and even in those early years there was rarely a great trial on the criminal side at which I was not present. I sat in a small compartment next the dock in Green Street when John Mitchel was sentenced in May, 1848, under the Treason Felony Act; and well do I remember the rush of men in the gangway near the dock, including members of the Bar, each one endeavouring to shake him by the hand before he disappeared for fourteen years.

In later years I was present at many important trials in the same court-house, in which my father took part as one of the counsel. Among these were that of Kirwan, for the murder of his wife on Ireland's Eye; the trial and acquittal of Father Petcherini, charged with burning the Bible outside the Kingstown Roman Catholic Church; and that of Spollen, for the murder of the Secretary of the Midland Great Western Railway at the Broadstone.

Whilst a law student I did not read, as was the custom then, with a member of the Bar. My father could not afford the necessary fee. This was largely compensated for by the indulgence of an old friend of my father's in the solicitor's profession, Mr. Thomas Geoghegan, who enjoyed a very considerable practice, and who allowed me to frequent his office for six months before my call. There I learned much of the practical work of the profession, and during my time with him prepared the brief which Mr. Geoghegan handed to Edward Gibson, afterwards Lord Ashbourne, lawyer, orator, and statesman, upon leaving the court on the day of his call to the Bar.

I sadly handicapped myself in the start by allowing nervousness to tie my tongue. Though a member for several years of the College Historical, the Legal and Historical, and the Law Students' Debating Societies (of the last I was secretary), I was never able to summon up courage to speak on any occasion except one. That was when I delivered a written judgment in the threadbare case of Lickbarrow v. Mason, overruling, to my own satisfaction at least, the decision of the majority of the English Judges who tried the case. Except on that solitary occasion, I had at the time of my call to the Bar never given utterance to my thoughts in public. I felt my disadvantage all the greater

when I witnessed the success of those who had
been fellow-students with me, but had continually
availed themselves of the opportunity of joining in
the various debates. I did not overcome the feeling of nervousness for two or three years after my
call. I did lose it gradually, but meanwhile, I fear,
valuable opportunity was lost.

I remember the first time I addressed a jury. It
was in Green Street. To use a common expression,
"I did not know whether I was standing on my
head or my heels." After the case was over a
friend who had been on the jury came to me and
said : " Mr. Curran, do you intend continuing at the
Bar ? Because, if so, my advice to you is to give it up ;
you will never do any good at it." I thanked him,
but replied : " I shall try, at all events." I did try,
and eventually found that, nervousness once got
rid of, I had a great facility for speaking, and on the
Home Circuit had great influence with the jurors.

In a book of reminiscences advice may be considered out of place, but I cannot help advising
young men about to make the Bar their profession
that they should at the earliest opportunity accus-
tom themselves to public speaking, and become
used to what at first is a most unnerving noise—
the sound of their own voice. This can best be
done in one or other of the debating societies. I
have often thought in the later days when fortune
smiled that few feelings are more pleasurable than
that of addressing a jury upon a complicated state

of facts, realizing as you progress that the initial hostility of those twelve good men and true is being gradually disarmed and the road smoothed to a favourable verdict.

While dealing with the art of public speaking, some few hints on cross-examination for the benefit of my many young friends of both professions will, I hope, not be considered out of place. Many of the most eminent of our Judges and of my professional friends at the Bar have commenced their legal career at Quarter Sessions, which forms a first-class school for beginners in either profession; and one who has presided over a County Court as long as I have may therefore presume to give the benefit of his experience.

In the first place, avoid shouting or speaking loudly to a witness unless you have caught him in a contradiction which you wish to emphasize. If the witness be apparently truth-telling, it only sets the jury against you out of sympathy for him. Some men—many, indeed, high in the profession—make a habit of commencing their cross-examination by taking the witness by question and answer through his direct examination, under the impression evidently that, if done in an unbelieving tone, this has the effect of shaking his evidence with the Judge and jury. It does nothing of the kind. In the vast majority of cases the repetition only sets up, by emphasizing, the evidence given on the direct.

It may be taken for granted that a considerable percentage of the parties charged with criminal offences are guilty. In defending a prisoner it is not his moral guilt that is at issue. The sole question for the jury is whether there is legal evidence to warrant a conviction ; hence it is always better, in cross-examining a witness whom you believe to be telling the truth, to steer as clear as possible outside the cardinal facts of the case, and to keep as much as you can to what I may call its fringe. This advice also applies to the case of a story concocted by two or more witnesses.

In the case of a witness who is apparently truth-telling, it would be better to rely on some discrepancy between the deposition and the evidence given in court, for such can nearly always be found. I have acquitted many upon such a discrepancy, purposely avoiding the main facts ; but it must be strongly relied on by counsel, otherwise the jury will not be impressed by it.

If a concocted story be supported by the evidence of two or more witnesses, they are certain to be positive as to their main facts, and to agree about them with little chance of being broken down by cross-examination. Here, again, one must keep clear of the evidence directly imputing guilt given on the direct, and deal only with the incidental evidence outside those main facts, relying only on apparently immaterial contradictions between the witnesses, and any difference between their statements and those in their depositions. I assume, of course, that a request has been made during the examination of each witness that all the other witnesses should be kept out of court.

On one occasion I defended a prisoner before Chief Justice Whiteside. My defence was that the case for the prosecution was grounded on the concocted story of the two Crown witnesses, and I relied on contradiction, one by the other, in their evidence on facts not material to the issue. In my address to the jury I called their attention to the case of Susannah and the Elders, which, though not admitted by all to be part of the Scripture, was at all events very ancient history. There the witnesses had, as here, been ordered out of court, with the result that, though agreeing in their concocted story, the Elders differed upon an apparently immaterial fact, the name of the tree under which the alleged offence had been committed, the result being the acquittal of the woman.

The Chief Justice, in charging the jury, said that such an argument could not apply in every case, as otherwise one might argue that the history of the crucifixion of Our Lord was false because the Gospels apparently differed as to whether both thieves were impenitent.

At all events, the jury considered the case of Susannah was good enough for them, and acquitted the prisoner.

I have always considered it unfair, in cross-examining a seemingly truthful witness, to try and break down his evidence by fastening on some mannerism or mode of speech, or his name. I only adopted this course on one occasion, and that was to some extent inadvertently. An employee of the Post Office was prosecuted before the late Judge Keogh for being short in his accounts. I defended the prisoner. The case for the prosecution depended upon the accuracy of a witness, who in a very clear manner showed the alleged defalcations. His Christian name and surname were very similar, and sounded almost alike. I shall call them A. B. I by mistake addressed him transposing the names. To the amusement of the jury, he indignantly denied that was his name. "My name, sir," he said to me, "is A. B., not B. A." I accordingly persisted in addressing him as Mr. B. A., with the result that he became so indignant that his evidence as to his accounts became confused and worthless.

It is well when you have to cross-examine a professional man, especially a doctor, upon a professional subject, to read up the matter the night before. Those gentlemen rely on their general knowledge acquired by practice, and also, I have often thought, upon the presumed ignorance of the lawyer on the subject, and frequently find themselves upset by questions as to the latest theories and practice found in the most recent textbooks. Knowledge thus acquired by me the

night before has often enabled me to break down
the evidence of a doctor on an important point,
both to his surprise and indignation.

I never scrupled about upsetting an official when
that was possible without doing the official any
injury. Mr. John Mallon, late Assistant-Com-
missioner of the Dublin Metropolitan Police, in
his " Recollections " edited by Mr. Bussy, gives
the following account of his cross-examination by
me : "Mr. Curran had defended a man named
Keenan, who was charged with shooting a land-
agent and solicitor named Cusack. I had been
called as a witness for the prosecution, and in that
case he gave me such a deuce of a hammering,
and so successfully turned and twisted my perfectly truthful evidence, that he won my admiration
and everlasting respect."

In cross-examination avoid as much as possible
asking a question when you are not fairly sure
what the answer will be. You may by asking such
questions recall to a truth-telling witness some
matter which he has inadvertently forgotten, or let
in evidence which could not have been given by
the Crown on the direct. It must be left to the
experience of counsel and having regard to the
necessities of the case to disregard this rule, but
in my experience its non-observance has resulted
in many a conviction.

You may cross-examine a witness as to the statements made by him in his deposition, but, as the

latter frequently contains illegal and prejudicial statements, do not read a part of the deposition to contradict him, or put it in evidence without first having ascertained the views of the Judge as to the law ; for some Judges hold that, if you read any part of it, it puts in evidence the entire of the deposition, whilst others, like the late Chief Baron Pigot, allow only the selected part to be used.

CHAPTER III

THE YELVERTON CASE—MR. WHITESIDE'S TRIUMPH

I was called to the Bar in the year 1860, and from that year, until he died in 1868, I was more than ever the constant follower of my father. Together with a dear old friend of mine a couple of years my senior, Constantine Molloy, of whom I shall speak later, I learned to discharge the most responsible duty which counsel can be called upon to perform—the defence of persons charged with crimes—by watching my father's peculiarly effective mode of cross-examination and address. But the crimes were not at that time of an ordinary description; most of them were murders, Whiteboy cases or similar offences, which arose from the troubled state of the country.

I remember one case tried before the late Chief Baron Pigot. A schoolmaster was tried before a jury in Maryborough on a charge of writing a threatening letter. The evidence as to the handwriting was very conclusive. An expert from Dublin, the late Mr. Power, then manager of the

National Bank, Mountmellick, and afterwards in College Green, and the District Inspector, all three, swore positively as to the identity of the writing in the threatening letter with a writing admittedly in the handwriting of the prisoner. The case for the defence seemed very hopeless. I need not say that my father in his address to the jury referred to the observation of Judge Keogh to the effect that " he would not hang a dog on the evidence of an expert." While he was speaking, knowing that our handwriting was very similar, I wrote my full name, " John Adye Curran," three times on a sheet of note-paper, and when he had concluded, asked him to write his name alternately after mine. This was done in the presence of Molloy. Mr. Power was then recalled, and having admitted that he was principally expert in signatures, having regard to his position in the Bank, he was asked if he could distinguish the handwriting in the six names on the sheet of paper. He requested some time to consider and consult with the other experts, and the Chief Baron agreed, and adjourned the Court for an hour. At the end of that time each of the three experts was recalled. Each differed one with the other, but not one was correct. Molloy was sworn as to the order in which the names had been written, and the prisoner was triumphantly acquitted.

The Right Hon. James Whiteside was a most accomplished and eloquent speaker and a splendid advocate. Not being overburdened with briefs for some time after my call, I had abundant opportunities of listening to him, and was an attentive spectator of his many triumphs at the Bar when in his prime.

I frequently followed him from court to court—but never alone, for, as his portly figure was seen emerging from a court, there might also be seen following in his wake a large crowd, who only waited to ascertain what court he next entered, once more to become his audience. All this continued as long as he remained practising at the Four Courts. He received a great and memorable ovation from all sides on his entry into the House of Commons after his magnificent speech in the Yelverton case. Very shortly after I was called, I felt greatly honoured by an introduction to him, and I sat behind him during the entire Yelverton trial.

With varying success, but final failure, Miss Teresa Longworth courageously fought her way through the various courts of England, Ireland, and Scotland, in the assertion that she was the lawful wife of Major the Hon. William Charles Yelverton, afterwards fourth Viscount Avonmore. She relied on two marriages—one in Scotland, where on April 12, 1857, the Major read aloud to Miss Longworth the Church of England marriage service in her lodgings in Edinburgh. They were afterwards married by a Catholic clergyman in the parish church of Rostrevor, Ireland, and lived together in both countries. The House of Lords eventually by a majority decided against the validity of both marriages. The matter came before the Irish Courts in the case of Thelwall v. Yelverton. The plaintiff claimed against the defendant, Major Yelverton, a large sum of money, for advances made by him to Miss Longworth as the wife of defendant. The case was tried by the late Chief Justice Monahan and a special jury in the month of February, 1861, and lasted several days.

There was a very strong Bar engaged on both sides. Mr. Sergeant Sullivan, Q.C., Right Hon. James Whiteside, Q.C., Francis Macdonough, Q.C., and John F. Townsend, LL.D., appeared for the plaintiff, instructed by Richard N. Parker, solicitor. The Right Hon. Abraham Brewster, Q.C., Mr. Sergeant Armstrong, Q.C., John Thomas Ball, Q.C., and H. P. Jellett, Q.C., appeared for the defendant, instructed by Messrs. Geale and Dwyer, solicitors.

The jury found for the plaintiff for the full amount, thus establishing the validity of the Irish marriage in Ireland. The announcement of the verdict was received with an extraordinary burst of applause from a densely crowded court. The cheers were taken up by an immense crowd which thronged the outer large hall and precincts, and by a still larger crowd which lined the quays for a considerable distance, and which had been from early in the day anxiously awaiting the result. The cheers were resumed again and again by the crowd, numbering over 50,000, as they accompanied the lady to the Gresham Hotel, and did not separate until she came out on the balcony, when she thanked them in some happy words.

I may add that the case had excited a great amount of interest in all parts of the United Kingdom.

One incident during the trial created a great sensation. A rather self-sufficient Englishman, and one who seemed to attach great importance to his testimony, had been examined on the part of the defendant, to prove that Miss Longworth had been seen by him at a certain place on an occasion which she denied. Mr. Whiteside proceeded to cross-examine him, and elicited from him the positive assertion that he could not possibly be mistaken, and that he was certain Miss Longworth was the lady he had seen. Having pinned him to the statement, the tall commanding figure of the great advocate was seen to lean back, as with his finger he pointed to the door at the left side of the Bench, and opposite to the side occupied by the witness. It was immediately opened, and there appeared in the doorway facing the Court and the witness a young lady, the very double of Miss Longworth—face, figure, hair, and dress, exactly alike. It was a scene to be remembered; the two ladies standing almost side by side, a smile of triumph on the face of Mr. Whiteside, and a look of consternation on the face of the witness as he glanced from one lady to the other. A dramatic dénouement truly when finally there came the admission that he could not say which of the two ladies was the one he had seen.

I never heard anything more able than the cross-examination of the defendant, Major Yelverton, by Sergeant Sullivan, afterwards Lord Chancellor, who was with Mr. Whiteside. The Sergeant by his first question—"Major Yelverton, did you love Teresa Longworth?"—placed the witness on the horns of a dilemma from which he was never able to extricate himself.

I was sitting in the Bar Bench behind Mr. Whiteside just before he commenced his noble and eloquent reply for the plaintiff. I observed, "We all expect a grand speech, Mr. Whiteside." With a sad smile he showed me a slip of paper, saying, "How can I?" I read on the note the words, "Come home as soon as possible, Mrs. Whiteside very ill—dying!" I think were the words. However, Mrs. Whiteside, though then critically ill, lived for some years longer.

Shortly afterwards the magnetic advocate became the majestic Chief Justice of the Queen's Bench. He frequently chose the dear old Home Circuit, and his good feeling towards all the members of that Circuit, and the enhanced measure of courtesy shown to them in the Queen's Bench, endeared the loyalty and sincerity of his character. I was at the time beginning to get into business on the Circuit, and probably out of affectionate memory of my father (who was then dead) he took every opportunity of showing me the weak and good points in my mode of speaking, giving me valuable advice which I afterwards utilized to advantage.

CHAPTER IV

THE OLD HOME CIRCUIT

WHAT sadness tinges all my memories of the old Home Circuit, which I joined in the year 1862, and which has ceased to exist for nigh thirty years. In former days and before railway accommodation was what it now is, members of the Home Circuit were accustomed to go from town to town on horseback. In after years they went by car. My father told me he drove frequently with Mr. John Dallas Edge, an old member of the Circuit. He was before my time, and was father of Mr. John H. Edge, K.C., ex-Legal Land Commissioner.

" May 1, 1885. Died on this date, the Home Circuit, aged 103 years, from exhaustion, and the result of an operation by the *Dublin Gazette.*"

So might run the epitaph of the old Home Circuit. Many of the most enjoyable years of my life were spent upon it, and its associations were dear to all who had the privilege of being enrolled among its members. The members were not very numerous, so it came about that it was more of a club than a Circuit in the ordinary sense of the word. The members were all close personal friends, each only too anxious to further the interests of his brother circuiteer, both off and on the Circuit.

An old gentleman named Walter Hussey Griffith was its Father during my earlier years. He was succeeded in the position by George Battersby, Q.C. Other members were John Thomas Ball, Q.C. (afterwards Lord Chancellor), Samuel Walker, Q.C. (afterwards Lord Chancellor), Edmund Bewley (afterwards Judge), Patrick Martin (afterwards M.P., Q.C.), Hamilton Smyth, Q.C., Edward Levinge (afterwards Judge in India), John N. Gerrard, Q.C., John H. Corballis, James Plunkett, James F. Martley, George Woods Maunsel, Leslie Montgomery, William F. Hort, John Alexander Byrne, Q.C. (afterwards police magistrate), Richard P. Carton (afterwards Judge), William O'Connor Morris (afterwards Judge), Loftus Fox, Charles D. Meldon, Q.C., and Francis Macdonough, Q.C. The last named, however, had left the Circuit before I joined.

Most, if not all, of the above stars—many of them very bright indeed—have set, but there is one of the brightest of them all still, we trust, high above the horizon. Such are the hopes of all who value strict impartiality, great learning, and splendid ability. I refer to the Lord Chief Baron Palles. There is a tradition on the Circuit regarding the first brief held by Chief Baron Palles. The brief was, as the tradition states, one to defend a prisoner at the Mullingar Assizes. Palles delivered an eloquent and impassioned address on behalf of injured innocence in the dock, and was warmly congratulated on his effort by his confrères. A voice from the gallery, whose owner's heart was clearly "in the dock," expressed his enthusiasm by a shout of "Bravo, Gossoon!" a startling act of contempt of Court, but one which at all events showed that his efforts had also been appreciated by the "gods." But tradition is silent as to what was the result to the prisoner. When a youth of sixteen I was in court with my father when the Chief Baron was called to the Bar, and I was also present when he was called to the Inner Bar.

Mr. Richard J. Meredith, K.C. (afterwards Master of the Rolls), joined the Circuit after I had left it.

The minutes of the Home Circuit after it had been abolished were lodged in the King's Inns Library by Mr. Constantine Molloy, Q.C., treasurer, and by Mr. John H. Edge, who had succeeded Dames Longworth as secretary. I may here mention that Mr. Edge's father, who, as I have said, was an old member of the Circuit, having joined at the same time as my father, unfortunately lost his life in the year 1844 while gallantly rescuing from drowning a young man who had fallen into the Grand Canal Harbour, Dublin.

I have been enabled to see the minutes contained in two large books. The earliest record, I find, is one of the year 1819, and in that the Home Circuit is treated as an existing Circuit. The names of those present at the Trinity Term meeting in 1830 are given; all of them subscribed to the rules. The following signatures appear:

Charles Ball, called in 1781.

Jonas Greene, called in 1790. This name subsequently appears as admitted in 1831. My former neighbour, the late Rev. Jonas Greene, B.D., was, I understand, a direct descendant of these two gentlemen.

Christopher R. Anticell, called in 1790, Father of the Circuit. It is supposed he was an original member with Messrs. Ball and Greene. The creation of the Circuit was about the year 1795.

Francis Blackburne, afterwards Master of the Rolls, Chief Justice of the Queen's Bench, twice Lord Chancellor, and finally Lord Justice of Appeal.

J. R. Corballis. He prosecuted round the Circuit, and succeeded Purcell O'Gorman as Assistant-Barrister for Kilkenny. It is related of him that Mr. Shortall, solicitor, being angry at one of his decisions, said : " I declare to God, I shall send to hell for Purcell O'Gorman and get him back here." This was the reply of the Judge : "I hope, Mr. Shortall, you will be your own messenger."

Arthur Bushe, Master of the Queen's Bench.

P. M. Murphy, Q.C., a great singer, who, it is said, sang himself at the Castle into the post of Assistant-Barrister.

Loftus H. Bland, Assistant-Barrister and Q.C.

Walter Berwick, afterwards Sergeant and Bankruptcy Judge. He was burned in the Abegele Irish Mail accident in the year 1868.

H. G. Hughes, afterwards Baron of the Exchequer.

CHAPTER V

CIRCUIT MEMORIES

I CANNOT remember a fraction of the stories of the splendid men who went the Circuit either as Judges or counsel, and so I am driven to tell a few which incidentally concern myself.

George Battersby, when Father, entertained a most unfriendly feeling towards the Leinster Circuit, to whom he was accustomed to refer as "The Forty Thieves." On one occasion I went to him to say there were two members of that Circuit in the town, and asking his leave to invite them to dinner. His reply was: "There is a public-house next the hotel; take them there and give them a drink."

Hans Hamilton, Q.C., was not very good in court, but was the best after-dinner speaker I ever heard.

The work on the Home Circuit at the time was fairly heavy, and John Thomas Ball was not very much inclined for work, especially during the summer days, and after dinner usually went up to bed about ten o'clock. At his request I followed him after a time, and, when I entered his room, found

him lying on his back in bed, a most striking figure
with his black hair on the white pillow. I then
read for him slowly each brief—there were always a
number—and left him at last to go to sleep. He
studied the briefs no more, but was thoroughly up
in the facts next morning.

The last night at Naas after the Assizes had
concluded was always a night of jollification. Each
man in the joy of responsibilities discharged was
at his best. There was plenty of good singing.
Samuel Walker, who had always command of a
sharp tongue, became concentrated vinegar, and
lashed forth at everyone, but ever with a saving
undercurrent of good nature—as was proved by the
uproarious laughter of all present, including the
individual who was being attacked.

Under the old Common Law Procedure Acts the
Home Circuit enjoyed many years of uninterrupted
prosperity. Notice of trial not served for the first day
of the after-sittings in Dublin would have to remain
over till the next sittings. On account of this a
venue late for the after-sittings was usually laid
in some town near Dublin, Naas being specially
favoured. I remember on one occasion there being
some fifty records for trial in that town. I lost my
chance on that occasion, being detained in Maryborough in the long case of Queen *v.* Moore, to
which I refer later.

But, alas! we had not taken into account the
jealous eyes of the Leinster Circuit, who really in

the transaction deserved the name applied to them by George Battersby. At the time Wicklow was the first town on their Circuit, and, though near Dublin, was too early in point of date to catch any of the stray venues. Then the wily Leinster men made Wicklow the last and not the first town in the Circuit list, and as Naas, the last town on our Circuit, was a mile and a half from Sallins, the nearest railway station, and the train ran right into the town of Wicklow, our little nest-egg was smashed. From that time the old Home Circuit commenced rapidly to decline. The big men had left it, and I recollect the last time I went round the Circuit, though I held a brief in every case, civil and criminal, I did little more than pay my expenses.

Baron Dowse often came the Home Circuit. On one occasion when he was the Judge I defended a prisoner in Maryborough, who was charged with an assault on a young girl. The evidence seemed very conclusive, my only defence being that she had not complained to her mother immediately, and I appealed to the common sense and knowledge of human nature of the jurors to discredit the case for the Crown. At that time I had considerable influence with the jurors in the several counties; and— as Dames Longworth once remarked to me—there was no use in prosecuting prisoners when I defended, as the jurors took the law and facts from me, not from the Judge.

The learned Baron laughed at my argument about human nature, and almost in words told the jury they were bound to convict. The jury after some time returned to court, and, to the astonishment of all, brought in a verdict of acquittal. The Baron seemed very angry, and told the foreman their verdict was in the teeth of the evidence. The facts were clear, and he had explained to them the law. " Well, your lordship," blurted out the foreman, " the jury preferred Mr. Curran's human nature to your lordship's law." I often afterwards used the same argument before Baron Dowse, whereupon the genial countenance of the learned Judge invariably lit up with a reminiscent smile.

Baron Dowse was very ready in repartee. In the old Law Library there was a small room opposite to the entrance which was chiefly occupied by some members of the Bar, highly Protestant in tone, and all good fellows. As I was passing the door one day I was called in and asked in a joking manner by one of them : " Curran, how is it that a Catholic will not eat meat on Friday, and will shoot a man down from behind a ditch on Saturday ?" I was thinking of some adequate reply, when I heard a voice behind me say (it was that of Baron Dowse, then Richard Dowse): " I will tell you, Foley : it is for the same reason that a good Protestant won't cook his dinner on Sunday, but will charge 500 per cent. on Monday."

No matter how busy the Baron might be when

at the Bar he was always ready to listen to any young barrister claiming his assistance on any matter of law or practice.

The Circuit never allowed the privileges of the Bar to be disregarded by the Bench, and upon the slightest infringement of them made plain their views. Chief Justice Whiteside's predecessor, Chief Justice Lefroy, who was a fine type of old Irish gentleman, and whose one delight was to have the young men round him, was on some rare occasions very curt and dictatorial to the members of the Bar in court. On one occasion Mr. George Battersby, Q.C., was pressing him on some point, when he refused further to hear him. On Mr. Battersby insisting, the Chief Justice told him in a peremptory manner to sit down. The same evening a resolution was unanimously passed by the Bar, binding its members not to appear in court before the Chief Justice unless he tendered an apology to Mr. Battersby. The resolution was conveyed to the Chief Justice through Mr. Courtney, his Registrar, with the result that next morning there was an ample apology in open court.

I was in Trinity College with Thomas Langlois Lefroy, his grandson, and years afterwards—in the year 1883—we renewed our acquaintance on the occasion of my going to Longford as Chairman of Quarter Sessions. Lefroy was a magistrate and Deputy-Lieutenant of the County, and constantly sat with me on the Bench. In his own house he was a most hospitable friend, and nothing could exceed his kindness to me when I was lying ill in Longford with an attack of peritonitis.

The old Chief Justice was a great temperance advocate. During one Assizes, when he was trying a case with a jury in Tullamore, a witness who said he was eighty-two years of age, and seemed perfectly sound and full of vigour, was asked by the Chief Justice if he was a temperate man. "I never touched a drop of liquor in my life, my lord," was his reply. With a smile of satisfaction, the Chief Justice turned towards the jury. "See, gentlemen," he said, "the result of what during my life I have always been advocating—temperance." The next was an old man equally strong and vigorous, and to all appearance as healthy. "I suppose you also," asked the Chief Justice, "have been temperate all your life?" Then, to the intense amusement of all the Court, except the Judge, the reply came: "Lord bless your lordship, for years past I have never gone to bed sober when I had a chance of getting anything to drink!"

The Right Hon. Michael Morris, afterwards Lord Morris, when Chief Justice, was another lover of the Home Circuit, selecting it, when he had the first choice, as "the liver wing, d'ye see."

There was one remarkable case tried by him in Tullamore with which I was intimately associated. A shopkeeper in that county, named Peter Claffy, paid some £500 for the interest in a farm to a man who pretended to be, but was not, the true owner. The latter shortly afterwards turned up in the person of a "returned American," named Michael Rigney. He brought an ejectment, the case was tried before Baron Dowse, and a verdict returned for plaintiff, and Claffy lost his £500. The plaintiff was afterwards sitting with his back to the window, at the wake of a friend, when a shot was fired from without, killing him instantaneously. Claffy, his brother, and two others were immediately arrested and sent for trial. The chief evidence against them was that of an approver.

The men were put on their trial on several occasions. Each trial, for various reasons, could not be proceeded with. So many delays had occurred that the Queen's Bench took the very unusual course in a murder case of allowing three of the men charged out on bail. Finally, Peter Claffy was tried alone before Mr. Sergeant Armstrong, the going Judge of Assize.

The case occupied a very considerable time. Constantine Molloy and I defended, and had alibi witnesses for each of the four men. All of these had to be examined, and, in addition, we had witnesses to prove an alibi for the informer. I occupied the greater part of the day in speaking to a great mass of evidence.

At about six o'clock in the evening, beginning to feel somewhat exhausted—it was a very hot day in August—I said to one of the Crown counsel sitting beside me, who I knew carried a flask, "Sam, give me a drop of brandy." He at once did so, and this tided me over another half-hour of strenuous speaking. Then again I asked him for a little more. His reply was : "I'll see you d——d first; if I did, you would keep us here all night."

Sergeant Armstrong charged very strongly for a conviction, but once more the trial proved abortive. The jury disagreed, and were discharged. This was the first time the case went to a jury. On a previous occasion the jury had separated during the trial, and they had to be discharged. On another occasion the principal Crown witness did not appear, and so the case dragged on until the next Assizes, when it came before Chief Justice Morris.

All the counsel dined with the Lord Chief Justice the evening before the trial, and after we had assembled he took me aside and said : "This case has become a grave public scandal, and I have determined to end it one way or the other. I hear you spoke for nine hours before Sergeant Armstrong. Now, I will give you three hours, and woe betide you if you exceed that time !" I took that as a plain hint that he was going to charge, if he could, for an acquittal, so I considered all I had to say, and concluded well within the three hours, holding the face of my watch towards him as I did so.

Strong as was the charge of Mr. Sergeant Armstrong for a conviction, equally strong was the charge of the Chief Justice for an acquittal.

When the jury had brought in their verdict of "Not guilty" there was some applause in court. The Chief Justice, slipping down from his bench towards a side gallery, pointed to a man sitting there, and told the police to arrest him and bring him before him. This was done, and the Judge immediately sentenced him to six months' imprisonment, for contempt of court in applauding, as an example to others. I interposed, and asked the Chief Justice to hear me for a moment. "No, I can't," he replied; "the public should know this place is not a theatre." "All the same," I pointed out, "you will change you mind when you hear me." "Well, what have you got to say?" "Only this, the man you have just sentenced to six months' imprisonment was one of the men out on bail, and had there been a verdict of guilty he would have been the next man to stand his trial for murder." The Chief Justice reflected for a moment, and then simply said to the man, "Go home."

Michael Morris, as Judge Morris, was at times kind and affable towards juniors in court, but frequently the very reverse. As Chief Justice he was on all occasions most gracious; every junior was sure of an indulgent hearing. I once nearly found myself in an awkward position as the result of this estimate of the Chief Justice, which I had mentioned to my friend Longworth Dames. Having expressed my views in this way, I thought no more of the matter, till one night at a Castle dinner the Chief Justice came up to me and said : "Curran, I hear from Dames you think that as Chief Justice I am a great improvement on what I was as simple Judge." I, needless to say, was somewhat staggered, and looked it. "You need not," he continued, "be angry with Dames, because I quite agree with what you told him. I feel in a much better humour with everyone since I became Chief Justice, and I always do my best for my young friends."

The following good story is told of Chief Justice Morris : The English Treasury had occasion to write complaining of the excessive use of coal in the offices of the Common Pleas in Ireland. Needless to add, the complaints did not interrupt the smooth tenor of the court. Some time afterwards the Chief Justice, when in his chamber, was informed by his tipstaff that a gentleman wished to see him. "Show him up," said the Judge.

The tipstaff thereupon ushered in a gentleman of very aristocratic appearance, who upon being asked his business, replied in a rather supercilious manner that he had come from the English Treasury with reference to the unanswered complaints as to the excessive use of coal. The Chief Justice made no reply, but calling in his tipstaff, told him that this gentleman was the coalman, and to take him down to the housekeeper, telling her who he was.

History is silent as to what the gentleman said

to the heads of the department when he went back, or whether they used less coal in the Court of Common Pleas from that day out. I never heard the result. History is also silent as to what were the feelings of the aristocratic Treasury clerk upon hearing himself described as "the coalman."

During my father's lifetime I was known on the Circuit as "young Curran." I regret, for obvious reasons, that that appellation would not fit me now.

I held my first brief on Circuit in the town of Carlow. It so happened that there was very little business anticipated, there being only one Crown case and no civil business. In addition to the Crown counsel there were only two members of the Bar present, both briefless barristers—the Hon. Henry Leeson (afterwards Lord Miltown) and myself. The solicitor consulted our old Bar waiter, Fox, as to which of us he should give the brief. Fox—I heard it all afterwards—at once said he thought I was the better man, though why he should have said so was a mystery to me. Anyhow, I got the brief, the prisoner pleaded guilty, and I managed to get him off with a light sentence. I received many a brief afterwards from the same solicitor.

For some years after I went the Circuit I paid my way by reporting for the *Irish Times*, *Freeman's Journal*, and *Saunders's News Letter*. At the time Circuit-reporting was done by members of the Bar, payment being at the rate of 10s. 6d. per day's report. In fine weather I invariably walked from town to town, as did many other members of the Circuit, the distance in no case exceeding twenty-five or twenty-six English miles.

Richard Gamble (afterwards Judge) reported for the *Daily Express*. He was a strong Protestant, and sometimes when busy asked me to report for him. Once in Carlow he came to me and said there was a nasty case against a priest, and he had to state the case, and had written out his speech, and requested me to send it to the *Express*. I said, All right, of course I should do as he wished; it was no affair of mine. On looking over the statement, I could see it contained rather strong language. He came to me before the case was called and told me that it had been settled, and not to send up his speech. I replied, I certainly should send it up, as I did not want to lose my 10s. 6d. (I need not say I never intended doing so.) He implored me not to send it up, and, after pretending to consider the matter, I said : "You have made very strong statements in it against a Catholic clergyman; I shall not report it provided you give me half a crown, to be handed by me to the most Catholic charity in Carlow." He willingly gave me the money., which I handed over to the Society of St. Vincent de Paul.

Edmund Meares Kelly was my father's senior at the Bar, and though old in years, was in point of health and spirits the youngest among us, and he was always willing to sit up with his juvenile friends to any hour at night for a game of cards. He was specially interested in the state of crime in the county Kildare, as he was one of the Crown prosecutors for that county. He also for years took a very active part in municipal matters in his own district.

At a dinner given by Samuel Walker to the members of the Home Bar after his elevation to the position of Lord Chancellor, some few of us remained chatting with him after the departure of many, including Mr. Kelly. At the joint request of all present, the Lord Chancellor promised to give him a silk gown, and this he did immediately afterwards.

In former times there were two permanent Crown counsel in each county, in addition to a number of supernumeraries, who were given briefs at the sweet will of the Crown Solicitor. One of the most generous in this practice was Stephen Seed, the Crown Solicitor for the county Kildare. However, the goose that laid the golden egg was eventually killed by a member of the Bar, a very decent fellow, but very vain, to whom I afterwards refer as singing, "My Pretty Jane."

Seed sent this member of the Bar, on one occasion, a third brief in a very small case. A consultation was deemed necessary, but the Crown Solicitor, thinking the Treasury would not stand the expense, did not call the third man in. The latter immediately wrote to the Attorney-General complaining of the Crown Solicitor's action, which he termed an insult. The result of this was that an inquiry took place, and an order was made that in future no briefs were to be given to super-numeraries unless specially directed. Thus many a Crown brief was lost to us poor juniors.

CHAPTER VI

SOME LEGAL MILESTONES—THE QUEEN *v.* MOORE

EVERY barrister who has been in any practice must have had at least one or two cases of outstanding interest. Some such cases I myself retain vividly in memory.

I received a brief from the solicitors to the Great Southern and Western Railway Company, at the Naas Assizes, to defend an engine-driver who had, with the porter at Sallins Station, been sent for trial for manslaughter. A man had been run over by the train, and the Company's case was that the porter was to blame in not giving the proper signal, and that the engine-driver was blameless. I was paid a fee of two guineas to journey down from Dublin on the engine (my first experience of travelling in such a position), so as to be able to see the signals on approaching the station. I made the case at the trial that it was the porter who had been the cause of the death, not the engine-driver, and the jury acquitted the prisoner.

I next defended the porter, my defence being that it was the engine-driver, and not he, who was the cause of the accident, and taking that view, the jury acquitted him also. My own opinion was that both were guilty of negligence, but the degree of negligence was not sufficiently culpable to warrant a conviction by the jury.

I did not take a brief to defend the porter without having first informed the railway solicitors of my intention, and obtained their consent; I also informed them of my intended line of defence. They raised no objection, but did not consider I should succeed. However, as I have already stated, I had at the time much influence with the juries. I may add, the case was tried before the late Chief Baron Pigot.

But on the Home Circuit I failed very distinctly on one occasion to influence them. It was when in one of the counties I defended a man for the abduction of a young widow. I had a very good defence, as in my cross-examination of the prosecutrix I made it appear that she was to a certain extent a consenting party. Unfortunately, it was known to the Judge, Chief Justice Whiteside, and to the jury, that my client was a leader of the Whiteboys in the county. The prisoner was convicted and sentenced to ten years' penal servitude; and, as I afterwards told the Chief Justice, my only consolation was that it took all his splendid oratory and ability in discussing the evidence to obtain a conviction. At the same time, I could not but feel that the county could well spare the prisoner for ten years.

Chief Baron Pigot was what is called a prisoner's Judge. He in this respect resembled Mr. Justice James O'Brien, uncle of the late Lord O'Brien of Kilfenora, who for several years was his Registrar, and came with him on the Home Circuit. Both Chief Baron Pigot and Mr. Justice James O'Brien did their best to help prisoners during their trial, but were very severe in their sentences in the case of a conviction.

A case which caused no little amusement was tried before Chief Baron Pigot at a Naas Assizes. His lordship was a very accurate note-taker, and as a rule took down both question and answer, and the raising of his pen with the words, " I am writing," was always a signal to counsel to pause in his questioning. As a rule he adopted the same practice in taking down cross-examination, destroying altogether in most cases its effect, especially in the case of an untruthful witness. At the request of the counsel he, however, sometimes ceased taking a full note so as not to give such a witness an opportunity of considering the answer he should give.

A soldier from the Curragh was being tried for larceny. The principal witness was an English sergeant-major, who seemed to have a high opinion of himself. In the evidence he deposed that he had seen the prisoner in the " A Square," pronouncing the letter with a strong aspirate. At the conclusion of his evidence the Chief Baron asked him at what hour he had seen the prisoner in the forage yard.

" I did not say I saw him in the forage yard."

" Is not that where you keep the hay ?"

" Yes, my lord."

"Well, you swore on your direct that you saw him in the hay square ?"

" I did not say hay square, my lord."

The Chief Baron reading, said, " Listen to your evidence taken down at the time : ' I saw the prisoner in the hay square.' "

" I did not say hay square, my lord ; I said (h)A Square."

It was some time before the matter was set right to the satisfaction of the painstaking Judge.

From time to time I have appeared in many important murder cases, but the longest of them all, and the one which attracted the greatest amount of public interest, was that in which James Moore was charged with the murder of a man named Edward Delany, near the town of Mountrath. The trial took place in Maryborough in the year 1873, before the late Chief Baron Pigot, and lasted seven weeks, during which time the jury, of course, had not been allowed to separate. The body of the murdered man had been found in a gulley by the side of the road. Various were the issues tried by the Chief Baron : one of them was on which side of the stream a man's hat had been found. The evidence became so complicated that the learned Judge drove out to Mountrath, a distance of seven miles, to investigate the matter at the place.

There were 114 witnesses examined in the case, and Constantine Molloy took two days in opening the prisoner's defence. I took five days speaking to the evidence ; but zealots for conciseness will not wholly condemn me when I add that the Solicitor-General, the Right Hon. Hugh Law, occupied seven days in replying for the Crown.

The Judge ; the Crown counsel, who were the Solicitor-General, Longworth Dames, Q.C., and Thomas Pakenham Law, Q.C. ; the solicitors for the Crown ; and for the prisoner Thomas Gerrard and Mr. Fitzsimons ; my dear friend and helpmate Constantine Molloy ; and the twelve jurors—are now all dead. I am the sole survivor ; the last of the jurors died lately.

Constantine Molloy and I considered our only chance was not to raise the issue of manslaughter ; nor was that alternative suggested by the Crown or the Judge, and the prisoner was convicted of murder and sentenced to death. After the conviction the condemned man used very strong language towards the Chief Baron, and wound up by saying that of the two he would survive the Judge, which proved to be the case.

After his sentence a memorial for reprieve was sent to the Lord-Lieutenant, backed by a statement signed by eleven of the jurors who convicted him, to the effect that, had they known they could have convicted him of manslaughter, they would have done so. His Excellency refused to interfere with the sentence. It was the late Lord Justice Barry who gave me the real particulars of the sequel.

The Chief Baron was lying ill, very ill, and he sent for Lord Spencer, and told him he could not die in peace or happy if the man were hanged; so, to the surprise of all, it was announced next day that his Excellency had reprieved the man, imposing a sentence of penal servitude for life. Moore died some years afterwards in a convict prison.

During my practice at the Bar I have defended in many murder cases, and I am glad to be in a position to write that in one case only was the extreme sentence of the law carried out against any of my clients.

At the Tullamore Summer Assizes of 1875 I defended a brother and sister, named respectively Lawrence and Margaret Shiels, for the murder of a man named Patrick Dunne, under very brutal circumstances. The male prisoner had been sentenced to six months' imprisonment for an assault on Dunne. Shortly after the expiration of the sentence the deceased was found in a deep drain alongside the road near Philipstown, suffering from two pistol-shot wounds, and with his throat cut. The cold water in the drain somewhat revived him, and his groans attracted the attention of a man passing by, who gave the alarm. The unfortunate man was at once removed to the local hospital, where he expired—surviving, however, a sufficient time to enable him to make a dying declaration, clearly indicating the two prisoners as his assassins. He also made the same statement to the man who found him on the roadside, and in the course of his statements used the expression, "Am I dying?" Our only defence was as to the sufficiency of the dying declaration, which constituted the entire case for the Crown.

Constantine Molloy was with me. The jury convicted both prisoners, and Chief Justice Monahan, who tried the case, upon our application, reserved for the Court of Criminal Appeal a question as to the sufficiency of the dying declaration.

When I was arguing the question, Chief Justice Whiteside, who presided, was pointing out to me the requisites for a valid dying declaration, when, without thinking, I said to him: "Of course, all

4

would be well and properly done if your lordship were making a dying declaration." " God forbid !" replied the Chief Justice, throwing up his hands, amidst much laughter. The court decided against us, and the two prisoners were afterwards executed in Tullamore Jail.

CHAPTER VII

A CIRCUIT POET LAUREATE—EXIT THE HOME CIRCUIT

IN the summer Assizes of the year 1855, members
of the Circuit, driving from Athy to Carlow, passed
through the village of Ballickmoyler, near which
was situated the residence of the dispensary doctor,
Dr. Bolton. When the waggonette, drawn by four
horses, was going past the doctor's gate, his children,
who were engaged tossing hay on the lawn in
front of the house, ran to it, thinking they were the
Judges, who were in the habit of going that way.
Foremost among them was a pretty young girl of
about sixteen years of age. "A real beauty, a real
Irish beauty, with raven-black hair and splendid
eyes"—the words are those of Mr. John H. Edge,
K.C., who knew the lady. As the waggonette
passed the gate, Mr. Stephen N. Elrington, who
was in it, saluted Miss Bolton by raising his hat.
The young lady smiled back in return, and, as it
afterwards transpired, was severely reprimanded
by her brothers and sisters for being so forward.

Mr. Elrington was a poet of no mean pretensions, and frequently delighted his fellow-members of the Circuit by singing and reciting his own compositions. That evening Elrington was late coming to dinner, and on being questioned as to what delayed him, he read the following ballad, composed by him while dressing, descriptive of the scene through which they had just passed, and which he afterwards often sang for the benefit of the Bar.

THE PRETTY GIRL OF BALLICKMOYLER.

I.

The sun had sunk behind the hills,
The sheep were 'mid the trees reposing,
The evening shades fell o'er the glades,
And Nature's eyes were softly closing.
We passed the quiet graves of Arles,
While weary birds were homeward flying;
The new-mown hay perfum'd the way,
E'en where the village dead were lying.
No more I sought than passing thought
To soothe my heart, sad wayworn toiler,
Till, luckless sight, I saw that night
The pretty girl of Ballickmoyler,
        The winsome girl,
        The witching girl,
The fairest maid in Ballickmoyler.

II.

Her bright black eye, its look so shy,
Her soft sweet voice, her smile so cheering,
Her raven hair and face so fair—
Was maiden ever so endearing?

Her gentle breast, where doves might rest,
So blest and free from life's vexations,
I frankly vow—my heart knows how
She gave it some quick palpitations.
What Irish boy could shun such joy,
Yet would of peace and fame despoil her?
Grow, blossom, grow; blow, young rose, blow,
Safe, 'mid the flowers of Ballickmoyler.
      The darling girl,
      The rarest girl,
The fairest maid in Ballickmoyler.

III.

How dull the years that intervene
'Twixt youth and nature's cold declining!
But sighing for what once hath been
Is only fruitless, vain repining.
Yet still those sheep-bells seem to ring,
Those shades to gather round earth's toiler,
And with light heart I still can sing,
"The Pretty Girl of Ballickmoyler,"
      The pretty girl,
      The rarest girl,
The fairest maid in Ballickmoyler.

I was at first under the impression that Chief
Baron Palles and my father were on the car, but
the learned Chief Baron informs me he was not,
and that my father could not have been on it, as
they always travelled together, and (the Chief
Baron adds) he distinctly recollects asking at dinner
that evening the cause of the merriment, and being
told of the scene in Ballickmoyler that day. The
Chief Baron is the sole survivor of those who were
present that evening, and for many reasons it is

very pleasant to find that his extraordinary memory corroborates my short history of that day and evening, now nearly sixty years gone by.

I had very recently the pleasure of meeting Miss Bolton, now Mrs. Cowell, the wife of my old fellow-student in Trinity College, the Very Rev. George Cowell, former Dean of Kildare. Time has not pressed heavily on her—she still, in fact, gives convincing testimony of the æsthetic appreciativeness of Mr. Edge.

Some few months after the Home Circuit had been abolished, a presentation was made to Mr. Elrington, accompanied by an address signed by every member of the Circuit then living. The address referred to him as the Poet Laureate of the Old Home Circuit, and expressed their grateful thanks for the many pleasant evenings he had afforded them for so many years.

The last Assizes of the existence of the Home Circuit was in the month of March, 1885. In opening the spring Assizes of that date in the town of Naas, Chief Justice Morris, in the course of his address to the Grand Jury of the county Kildare, said :

" There was another matter he thought it becoming he should allude to, as this was the last town of Assizes on the Home Circuit, a Circuit which, having gone many and several times, it had been his privilege to select as the going Judge of Assize. They were no doubt aware that the Home

Circuit had been abolished. Called into existence 103 years ago, it had been now thought right in the public interest that it should be abolished. He thought, under the circumstances, that it was becoming that he should take farewell of it. He did this with the more regret when he remembered how often he had gone on it, and enjoyed the society and assistance of such a very learned Bar as it boasted—a Bar which had sent a reasonably sufficient quota to the Bench and the highest places in the administration of justice—a Bar which, he might say, included a Blackburne, a Hayes, a Brewster, a Hughes, a Palles, and a Ball, and which at that moment included a gentleman quite entitled to be ranked with those—Mr. Walker, Solicitor-General for Ireland, who might be considered as occupying a high step on the ladder to the Bench."

The Circuit had a very large quantity of valuable plate, which was divided among its members when it was broken up. Unfortunately I did not share in the division, as very shortly before I had been appointed Divisional Magistrate. However, I am not quite without a relic of old times, as my friend Archibald J. Nicolls, who was a member at the dissolution, gave me a portion of his allotment. At the same time, I know that had I pressed the matter I should have been given my share.

I dined as a guest with the Bar at its last dinner at Naas in March, 1885. A resolution was then passed to divide the property among the existing members, with a special addition that a memento of the Circuit should be given to Longworth Dames and myself. With the consent of all present, I took the old snuff-box made of some composition, with the inscription on the outside, "Home Bar." This, with the silver given to me by Mr. Nicolls, I am very proud of, and I have always treasured both among my dearest possessions.

CHAPTER VIII

SPORTING AND SOCIAL INTERLUDES

SINCE I have taken up my pen to lighten the tedium of retirement and while away those hours which for years were occupied by the concerns of my clients or devoted to the duties of my court, I have been bewildered by the medley of reminiscences stored away in my memory. Personalities, stories, incidents and cases, are entwined in such an annoying entanglement that it has become wellnigh impossible to sort them, or to place them under chapter headings. However, I must only do my best. I shall say my say, and whenever it occurs to me that your patience may tire, I shall break with a new chapter.

Sport and exercise of all kinds ever appealed to me, and long walks often from town to town upon Circuit kept me in that state of physical fitness which is so essential in those who follow the law. On one occasion a member of the Circuit, by name John Hickey, afterwards in the Land Commission, was boasting at dinner of his running powers. After listening to his boasts, I said I would back myself

for £2 against him.   We arranged the race should
be for 100 yards, and be run in the Phœnix Park.
That the race was to come off was soon known in
the Library, and a pretty good muster from court
came to see the fun.   Hickey appeared rather late,
and in his hands I saw a pair of spiked racing shoes.
I objected, but he retorted that there was nothing
said in the bet about shoes.   He sat down and
proceeded to put one of them on, and, while he was
doing so I sat down and put the other on, saying
we should be evenly matched with one spiked shoe
on each.   After some hot words I had to give back
the shoe.   At length we started, and, as I expected,
I, in racing terms, "romped home" a long way
ahead.   I don't think I demanded the stake
money.

Flat racing never appealed to me very much, but
I delighted in watching a good steeplechase, and so
Aintree and Punchestown found me a very frequent
visitor.   A somewhat unpleasant experience with a
most pleasing termination was the result of one of
my visits to Aintree.   I was walking in the carriage
enclosure with a friend from Dublin, when I suddenly felt a hand in my breast pocket.   On looking
down it disappeared and its owner immediately
made off.   I followed at once, but was tripped up
and brought to my knees by a confederate.

When I regained my feet I saw the thief dis-
appearing behind a carriage, and I continued the
chase, and kept him in view as he dodged round

the vehicles until he took to the open, where I easily ran him down, and a struggle began. I was handicapped at first by having an umbrella in my hand, but this I threw over to my friend, who was on the outside of a large crowd which had assembled and stood round us, not interfering. We came to the ground several times, but, up or down, I never let go my grip of his arm and coat. When nearly exhausted, I was relieved by seeing a big burly man elbowing his way through the crowd towards us. He asked me what was the matter. On ascertaining that he was a constable, I told him I had caught the man's hand in my pocket as he was trying to steal my watch. The constable said to me, " He has succeeded," and looking down I saw my chain hanging without my watch.

The constable then took the man into custody and asked me to follow him to the police-station under the grand-stand. The charge having been made, I was directed to attend the next day (Saturday) to prosecute before the magistrate in Liverpool. I said I could not possibly do so, as I was a barrister and held a brief in a record in Dublin, which was first on the list on that day, and that I intended going home at once so as to appear in it. The constable then informed me that the prisoner was a most expert thief, and that that was the first occasion they had been able to catch him, though long on the look-out. In the end they prevailed upon me to stay.

I had to wire to my solicitor in Dublin apprising him of my inability to be present next day, with the result that I received no more briefs from him for a considerable time after. At the hearing next morning I refused to come back to prosecute at sessions, and, after I had given my evidence, the prisoner under some local Act was sentenced to six months' imprisonment.

My next move was to keep the matter out of the Dublin papers, but in the case of one of them I did not succeed. Some reporter in Liverpool wired to that paper on Saturday the full account of the case, giving my evidence in full, including that of my struggle with the thief.

Shortly after my return home my wife was told not to allow me to buy another watch, as some of my barrister friends were about presenting me with one; and from some thirty of them I received a beautiful gold watch, bearing the following inscription :

" To John Adye Curran, from a Few of his Many Friends at the Bar. April, 1877."

The late Mr. Justice Murphy, who was then at the Bar, came to me when he heard of the presentation, and complained that he and a great number of the members of the Bar had not been told of it, or they would have been only too happy to have joined.

That charming actor and prince of bonhomie, Edward Terry, was a friend of mine of many years'

standing, and he invariably wound up all his visits to
Dublin by coming to my house in Gardiner's Place
for supper after the performance in the theatre.
I had there to meet him many members of the Bar,
some of whom had splendid voices.   Terry was
always delighted with "Bonnie Dundee" of Longworth Dames (afterwards Dames Longworth), with
the "Pour out the Rhine Wine" of James Rynd,
and with the singing of Arthur Houston, who had
indeed a beautiful voice.   I remember having
among us, too, a tall and graceful young man, who
afterwards blossomed into the distinguished personality of the late Lord Justice Moriarty.

One night a member of the company who was
very vain of his singing, and fond of sentimental
songs, was called upon for a song.   He threw
himself into what he considered an impressive
attitude and commenced, "My Pretty Jane."   On
hearing the voice, my children, who had been
outside the door listening to the singing, commenced to titter and ran away.   A young barrister who has since attained to one of the highest
positions on the Irish Bench, and who was sitting
facing the open door, seeing and hearing what
was taking place outside, was also unable to
avoid laughing.   The singer stopped and, looking
at him sternly, said : "Sir, you are no gentleman."

"Never mind, Peter," said Richard Adams
(afterwards County Court Judge of Limerick) from

the other end of the table, "he thought you were singing a comic song." The singer did not seem to be very rapturous over the form of consolation.

On these festive nights Terry came out in his best form, and gave us song for song, many of them never having been sung in public. With those whom I have mentioned, the following also generally helped to form the party : The present Master of the Rolls, George Wright (afterwards Justice Wright), Jehu Matthews, George Perry, his brother Jeremiah Perry, A. J. Nicolls, Henry Treacy, Alexander Lane, R. Peebles, Edward O. McDevitt, and Richard P. Carton (afterwards Judge). The last-named left one night early, protesting that he had some work to do, but in about half an hour returned, saying he could not stay away from the fun.

The gentleman who sang "My Pretty Jane" —he was a member of the old Home Circuit— was very vain of his powers as an advocate, and considered that he had been improperly passed over by the preferment of others less deserving. Nevertheless, he was a great favourite on Circuit, affording amusement as well as pleasure to us all.

CHAPTER IX

INTER-CIRCUIT COURTESIES—THE CLITHEROE
CASE—MR. JOHN REA AND THE TEMPER-
ANCE PARTY—REVISION WORK

MY pride as a member of the Home Circuit was
not so overweening and arrogant as to deny myself
the hospitality and courtesy of other Circuits when
offered. I remember many years ago spending two
very pleasant nights with the members of the
North-East Circuit at Dundalk.

I went down to prosecute for the Harbour
Commissioners a former employee who had robbed
them to a considerable amount by an ingenious
system of book-keeping. It had taken me weeks
to study the accounts before I discovered his mode
of procedure, and was able to frame an indictment. The prosecutors considered it necessary
that I should attend as counsel at the Assizes,
and I arrived the night before the trial. The
next day I could only in part reap the fruits of
my industry, because the prisoner, under the advice of the late Judge Monroe, who defended him,
pleaded guilty.

63

I was most hospitably entertained by the Circuit on each of the two nights. As I had arranged to go up by the night mail on the second night, the greater number of the Bar determined to sit up with me until I started. I had often spent many pleasant nights on the Home Circuit, but never one pleasanter than this. John McMahon, Andrew M. Porter (afterwards Master of the Rolls), Walter Boyd (afterwards Judge), John Monroe (afterwards Judge), and many other members of the Circuit, kept that jolly vigil with me. During the evening one of the party said he was sorry he could not wait up any longer, and left saying he had some work to do. He reappeared about an hour afterwards, and to our great amusement said he had been hunting up and down through the town, and had been unable to find his lodgings. In the end I gave him the room I had taken for myself.

Speaking of the North-East Circuit reminds me of Clitheroe's case. I had the honour not only of starting that case before the late Recorder of Dublin, Sir Frederick Falkiner, but of arguing upon every aspect of it, and appearing for every class of person affected by the ultimate decision. I am not going to take up space with the legal question at issue more than to say it very vitally interested the rights of assignees of ordinary licences. Not only is the case an example of the curious vagaries of professional life not easily to be understood by the layman, but it shows the treatment which is often meted out by a busy senior to an industrious junior.

I appeared for the Licensed Grocers' and Vintners' Association ; and, after hearing me, the Recorder, having regard to the magnitude of the case, said he should have the matter fully argued by counsel on both sides. Mr. Macdonough was briefed to appear with me ; and, at his request, I went to his house and spent a couple of hours putting my views before him and going over the various statutes bearing on the case. Before leaving I mentioned one small point, saying that I did not think much of it, but might as well mention it, which I did. When the case came on again for argument both sides were fully represented. Mr. Macdonough went thoroughly through all the points I had put before him, of course far more ably than I could have done, and wound up by saying, to my utter astonishment, " There is one argument to which my friend attaches great importance, but I do not consider of much value." He then proceeded to state the argument which I had previously told him in consultation I had thought of little or no weight.

That his course of action had been thoroughly understood by the counsel on the other side I saw clearly by the smile passing across the face of Sir Andrew M. Porter, who appeared for the Crown.

At the conclusion of my argument on the first day Mr. T. W. Russell, now President of the Local Government Board, who then represented the Temperance party in Dublin, asked me would I have any objection to go down to Newry Quarter Sessions next day and argue the same point on the Temperance side. I went and combated all my arguments of the previous day with success.

While in Newry a deputation from Belfast came to me and requested me to go there next day before the Recorder, Mr. Ottway, and argue for the grocers and vintners in that city; so I went and repeated my Dublin argument there, and tried to upset all the arguments I had used in Newry.

I spent a week in Belfast, a very pleasant one. I had opposed to me the celebrated John Rea, representing the Temperance party. He could use strong language; so could I. We both did use it, but we parted the best of friends, and he never afterwards came to Dublin without calling me in the library to have a long chat.

During the course of the case Mr. Ottway wrote me down a note in the following words: "Are you a son of my old friend John Adye Curran? If so, I congratulate you." I never could make out whether I was congratulated on being my father's son or on account of the ability of my arguments.

It was all through my life to my advantage to be known as my father's son, for I was always receiving evidence of the esteem in which he was held. He represented for many years the Inn's Quay Ward in the Corporation, first as town councillor and afterwards as alderman. He filled the latter position until his election as Legal Assessor. At his death I was elected to succeed him in that post, and I had to face a spirited contest, in which I was opposed by two brother barristers, one a Conservative, the other a Liberal. All the Judges voted for me, and I remember the late Sir Dominick Corrigan, an old friend of my father's, brought up many voters. I remarked one gentlemen working the greater part of the day, whom I afterwards discovered to be Judge Newel Barron, Q.C., another friend of my father's. Mr. Charles Barry (afterwards Lord Justice) sat beside me at the declaration of the poll, and I was elected by a large majority over the other two combined. My colleague was Mr. James M. Hyndman, who was succeeded by Mr. Hart.

I held the position for fourteen years, the pay being one hundred to one hundred and twenty-five guineas for three weeks' work. Under the present law the Burgess Roll and the Parliamentary lists are identical, and are settled by the Parliamentary Revising Barristers.

Under the municipal law barristers were competent to appear at the revision of the Burgess Roll. The Liberals were invariably represented by a very small gentleman, by name Thomas Reid (not so long gone from amongst us), who had an intimate knowledge of the pecuniary position of every man on the roll. He was very clever, but his education was not up to the level requisite for his position. I remember him greeting a doctor on his appearance at the door, before he had advanced a yard into the court, with the observation, "The ould complaint, doctor, the ould complaint!" The doctor had not been in the habit of paying his rates regularly, and we had to strike his name off for non-payment that year.

The Conservatives were usually represented by a junior barrister, and sometimes by the late Mr. John Byrne, a very able man, and the language passing between the latter and Reid was not always that of the old-time equity practitioner.

One year Walter Boyd, now Mr. Justice Boyd, then a young barrister, represented the Conservatives, and had been pressing on us the doctrine of "idem sonans." I still have before me his look of indignation and disgust when Reid, in replying, referred to him as his "learned friend," and emphatically dissented from his reading of the doctrine of "sidem sonans."

During my election contest I employed Reid. One day he came to me and said he wished to be absent next day, as he had to go down to Sligo to vote at an election. "I never knew you had property there or anywhere," I said. He then informed me that as the law then stood, a claim to vote as a freeholder, when not objected to, gave the claimant his vote ; and, as no one appeared to know whether or not to object, in that way he was a voter in several counties in Ireland. He also informed me that he had been sent a first-class return ticket by the Conservative agent. "I did not know you were a Conservative," I then said. "Oh no!" was his reply, "I am going down to vote for the Liberals." I endeavoured to dissuade him from going, but he left me, asserting his intention to go down. The next day but one he appeared, looking very sick and sore, and told me he had got a most unmerciful beating.

It appeared that a body of police met the voters at the train, and escorted them amidst booing and hooting, to the booth, where they waited to escort them to the hotel. Reid, being a conspicuous figure, came in for a particular share of the crowd's attention. Unfortunately it was open voting, and when, to the surprise of all, he voted for the Liberals, the Conservative agent took hold of him and shot him out into the crowd. The crowd, being then under the impression that he had voted with those who came with him from the train, escorted by the police, and not crediting his cries that he had voted for the Liberals, left him to go back in the train very repentant, sad, and sore.

I frequently advised and acted for the Royal Irish Constabulary and the Dublin Force, both officers and men, and also for medical men, but invariably refused to take fees from any of them. My usual advice to officers and men who were in controversy with their superior officers was to "knuckle under." My experience of many such disputes showed me that no matter who was right or who was wrong, the inferior always came to grief badly. A superior will never admit any error.

I was consulted once by two young constables as to their defence in a prosecution against them for a bad assault on a civilian. They had been sent for trial, and I had appeared for them before the then Chief Magistrate. They were out on their own bail. I was satisfied they would be convicted and receive a heavy sentence, and told them what lay before them.

They said they had friends in America. I declined further to advise them, and said they must act as they thought best. The next I heard was that both had left for America. Shortly afterwards I received a letter from one of them enclosing my fee of two guineas. This I had refused to take. My solicitor also received a remittance.

I doubt very much if any member of the Bar has had an experience similar to the following. A Coroner's inquisition, to hold water, requires to be very carefully drawn. It has no friendly Act of Parliament, as have indictments, to aid it. During the bad times of the Land League a process server, guarded by a sergeant and two constables of the Royal Irish Constabulary, was seen advancing along the public road some three or four miles distant from Ballaghadereen. Immediately all the bells and horns in the neighbourhood were sounded, and in a short time a very considerable body of men armed with sticks and stones faced the police. Their attitude became so threatening that the sergeant, after warning them, gave the order to fire, with the result that one of the crowd was shot dead. Before the men had time to reload the crowd rushed in on them, and a mêlée ensued. The two constables and the process server escaped, but the sergeant was so badly beaten that the injuries resulted in his death.

The inquest on the man who was shot was held by the Coroner—an old gentleman named McDonough—in a school-house on the mountain-side near the spot where the affray had taken place. I appeared for the next-of-kin, and William S. Bird, afterwards Judge, appeared for the police, instructed by the Crown Solicitor.

The investigation lasted three days and necessitated a drive from Ballaghadereen (where I was staying) and back each day. The police had to walk the same distance. We had two cars, and on the last evening I offered Mr. Burke Irwin, then District Inspector, afterwards Resident Magistrate, a seat on one of them, but the driver point-blank refused to allow him up, and I had to smuggle him on to my car without the knowledge of the carman.

After the evidence and speeches had closed, I took a stroll along the road, and on my return was astonished to hear that the Coroner was in with the jury—a most improper proceeding. After some time he sent me word that he and the jury wanted to see me. At first I refused, but yielded to a second message, as I considered that, having regard to the presence of the Coroner with them, my presence could do no additional harm.

When I entered, I informed Mr. McDonough that his action had vitiated the entire proceeding, and that no verdict of the jury could stand in law. He replied that the jury were bringing in a verdict of " Wilful murder " against the two constables, and all he wanted to know was whether the inquisition had been properly drawn up. After reading it I saw that it was open to every objection such a document could show, and so I told them. I was then requested to draw up a proper form, and, upon asking for another sheet of parchment, was informed that the Coroner had only brought one. I then took the one he had used, drew lines across the first finding, and wrote a proper form of inquisition for wilful murder on the other side. I then informed Mr. McDonough that the entire matter was a fiasco, and that he should not act upon a verdict so obtained. " On the contrary," he replied, "I shall issue my warrant to arrest the two men and have them lodged in Sligo Jail to-night." "Will you?" I thought to myself.

On leaving the jury-room, I said : "Don't come out for about a quarter of an hour after me, as people might think I had been settling your verdict." On emerging, I sidled up to Bird and told him what had occurred, and advised him to get the two men out of harm's way. This he immediately did, and they were soon on their way to Sligo, but not under the Coroner's warrant. Shortly afterwards the Coroner and jury appeared. The Coroner announced the verdict, and handed a warrant for the immediate arrest of the two constables to the District Inspector, who informed him it could not be executed, as the men were not present. They were not seen afterwards until in the Queen's Bench on an application for bail.

My real clients were the men charged with the murderous assault on the sergeant, and these men had been sent for trial. I considered the verdict against the constables quite sufficient for my purpose without incensing the Crown (who were very tender about matters affecting the police) by the public arrest of the two constables. The result proved my views to be correct. No application was made by the Crown to set aside the inquisition, and I consented to forego my rights under it and not to ask to have the men tried, on the condition that the Crown should drop the prosecution of the men charged with the assault. The Crown Solicitor, knowing what I had done at the inquest—in preventing the arrest of the constables—met me more than half-way, and assented, so the matter ended.

CHAPTER X

THE POLICE AS WITNESSES

I HAVE almost invariably found that the police, considering the difficulty of their position, especially in Ireland, in obtaining evidence in the various cases in which they represent the public, and the temptation to supplement testimony by imagination, discharge their duty with commendable fairness. They are often honestly mistaken, like any other human being, as the following incident will show.

Previous to the act of conferring jurisdiction, in the case of malicious injuries, on the County Court Judges, an applicant for compensation had to go first before the Presentment Sessions and then before the Grand Jury. A gentleman whose house and premises had been, as he alleged, maliciously burned, applied to the Presentment Sessions in a district of the county Dublin. I appeared for him, and when I alighted from the train the District Inspector—or, in the title of that period, the Sub-Inspector—met me and told me I could do no good, and might return home, as they had evidence

75

that my client had admitted he burned the place himself.

This statement rather astonished me, and I asked my client about the matter. He indignantly denied ever having made such an admission. A young constable was examined, and swore that, in conversation with the applicant, the latter had informed him that he had burned the premises himself. The officer was rather stupid, but was evidently telling what he believed to be the truth, and I at once saw how the mistake had arisen. I put it to him : Did he first ask him the question, " Was it you burned the place ?"

" Yes," he replied ; "I told him I thought he must have burned it himself, and asked if that was the fact."

" Was it then he said he set the place on fire ? In answer to you did he say, ' I burned it ' ?"

" Yes, those were the words he used."

" Did he speak the words in a loud manner ?"

" Yes."

Then I repeated the words, laying an emphasis on the " I," and asked, " Was that the way ?"

" Yes," he replied.

It was thus quite evident that the constable took the astonished query of the applicant for an admission, and my client, having been sworn, stated, when asked if he had himself set fire to the place, that he did use the expression, but with a strong emphasis on the " I "—astounded by the charge in the suggestion. My client was afterwards allowed compensation by the Grand Jury.

It is hardly necessary to observe that the police contribute their full share of the amusing incidents which lighten and leaven the course of justice. A prisoner charged with the offence of manslaughter was tried before the late Baron Fitzgerald at the Commission Court, Green Street. I defended him. The case occupied the day, and at six o'clock the jury, after a short absence, came into court and intimated to the Judge that they could not agree. His Lordship said it was too soon to discharge them, as the case was an important one, and told them that he should return at nine o'clock. As there were no bailiffs in court, a young constable was put in charge of them and sworn not to allow them to separate or allow anyone to communicate with them. We all returned shortly before nine, and were astonished to find one of the jurors sitting alone in the front of the box and the constable some distance behind him. The Baron was very angry, and asked the constable why he had disobeyed his orders as to allowing the jurors to separate.

" My Lord," said the frightened young man, "you swore me not to speak to them, or allow anyone to speak to them, and so I could not tell the juror to go back, and could do nothing but follow him out."

The learned Judge twisted round, took a pinch of snuff, and told him to call out the remaining eleven jurors.

On one occasion I happened to be in a Petty Sessions Court in the county Dublin, before a full bench of magistrates. A man was being charged with having assaulted a constable who was a rather small man, and with having used bad language. "The words were so bad," added the witness, "that I don't like repeating them." One of the magistrates, a fiery, peppery little gentleman, insisted on the words being repeated, and threatened to report the constable unless he did as he was ordered. Some of the other magistrates considered it was not necessary, but the little gentleman still insisted on his rights.

"You be damned, you dirty little devil!" suddenly blurted out the constable.

"How dare you, sir, address such language to me? I shall certainly report you now," shouted back the peppery little gentleman, ablaze with indignation.

It took some time before his worship could be convinced that the words which he thought applied to himself were those he insisted on the constable using.

CHAPTER XI

THE BAR AT HOME AND ABROAD—MR. JUSTICE WILLS—ISAAC BUTT

RECIPROCITY and good-fellowship seem to be out-standing characteristics of the Bar wherever it exists. Witness the splendid reception accorded to the Father of the Irish Bar, the late Hyacinth Plunkett, K.C., in France some few years ago.

I myself can speak from experience of the same kindly feeling existing among the Belgians. When a young barrister I happened to be in Brussels, and wandered into the Law Courts, which were sitting at the time. On entering, I went up to a member of the Bar, and, telling who and what I was, requested him to show me the various courts. He immediately consented, and I spent a very pleasant half-hour in his company.

He finally brought me into a court where a number of Judges were sitting at a horseshoe table, the members of the Bar facing them. I went with the young advocate down to the front row, where I sat for a short time. While there I saw the Judge who sat in the centre, and who appeared to be the Chief, send a note to my friend. The latter told me that the Chief was asking who I was, and that he had replied on a note stating I was an Irish barrister. The Chief Judge read the note, and then passed it round to the Judges on either side of him. To my confusion and astonishment, the Chief presently stood up and made me a most profound bow. Immediately afterwards all his colleagues also stood up and bowed to me. Making a sorry attempt at an appearance of self-possession, I rose at once and returned the salute. When leaving the court, I bowed again, and this salute was ceremoniously acknowledged by the members of the Court.

I had a similar experience in Scotland, when travelling in that country with some friends, including the late Judge Adams. Adams and I were both young barristers at the time, and of course we went to see the Law Courts, which were then sitting. Walking through, we spoke to a Scottish barrister, who, at our request, brought us round and showed and explained all that was to be seen and visited, including the refreshment-rooms. In fact, the title of "Irish Barrister" seems to be an invaluable passport, both at home and abroad.

On one occasion, at the Assizes in Liverpool, when there was an important case on trial in which the public took a great interest, I tried to get into the court, but was informed by the constable at the door that I could not possibly enter, as the court was crammed and there was no room for any more people. I said to him: "Could you get me in? I am an Irish barrister." To the disgust of all those waiting outside with me, he not only let me in, but gave me an excellent place. Perhaps the worthy fellow was a compatriot. In any case he clearly acknowledged me as a brother "limb of the law," and as such entitled to preferential treatment.

Some few years after I had been called to the Bar I was standing in the hall of the Four Courts, in my wig and gown, when a stranger came up to me, and, telling me he was a member of the English Bar, asked me to show him round the several courts. This I did, pointing out by name each of the Judges. When we came to the Court of Common Pleas, he said he knew Chief Justice Monahan, and would like to see and speak to him. It was then about the time for adjourning, and when the Chief Justice had retired I brought the stranger to his chamber. When parting, he asked me my name. I gave it to him. "A very good name for an Irish barrister," he said. I then asked for his name, and his answer was, "I am an English Judge, and my name is Wills." He then shook hands with me, and I said: "I may bear a great name, but you have made one."

One should have, as the saying goes, "one's wits about one" in defending prisoners during the years

6

Mr. James Murphy, Q.C., and Mr. William O'Brien, Q.C. (both afterwards Judges), prosecuted. I can speak from experience that both gentlemen were very strong prosecutors, and in very few cases omitted replying for the Crown. In court those two strenuous Crown counsel and I, who was then defending prisoners, would appear the bitterest of antagonists; outside court we were the best of friends, and as such we finally parted.

The late Mr. William O'Brien, Q.C., who when a Judge showed rare eloquence in his considered judgments, notably that on the Erasmus Smith endowed schools, was also very quick at repartee. On one occasion when in the library, Four Courts, he asked the late Judge Webb to sign some application. He told Webb the contents of it, but said he had not time to let him read it.

"I never sign what I do not read and understand," replied Webb. Quick came back Judge O'Brien's reply:

"Yes, you do—pleadings."

One little story of the great Isaac Butt must conclude this chapter. I had not any opportunity of being personally acquainted with him, until a few years before his death. He was at the time living in the house bought for him in gratitude for his services, in North Great Georges Street. He was very lonely and apparently deserted by his friends. I lived in Gardiner's Place close by, and at his request I frequently called down to chat with

him in the evening. He was a great advocate. I
heard him defending Kirwan, who was convicted
of murdering his wife on Ireland's Eye, and I was
much impressed by his great ability as a speaker—
as were all who were present. He was remarkable
not only for his great eloquence in addressing juries,
but for his impressive style in addressing the Court
upon matters of law.

He could command any amount of work ; nevertheless he was always in money troubles. He
seemed to have no knowledge of the value of money.
The late A. M. Sullivan told me that on one occasion there was an action for libel against the
Nation newspaper to be tried at Wicklow Assizes.
Mr. Butt was retained for the defence, and the
venue being off his circuit, a cheque for one hundred
guineas was sent with his brief. He returned the
cheque, saying he was very indignant that they
should imagine he would ask any fee in such a case.
He went to Wicklow, but on his way to the train
called at the *Nation* office and changed a cheque of
his own for ten pounds. " No funds " was the reply
of the bank.

He had a remarkable habit when addressing
the Court or a jury of twisting in his thumb
and forefinger a penknife, holding it by the open
blade.

Mr. Butt, like many other great men, did not
shine in small cases of no public interest. His
great mind soared above such matters. Witty,

warm-hearted, off-hand and generous, one thought
he would have led the Irish people, of whom he was
typical, to the end.   Dethroned by his antithesis,
that mysterious and awesome personality with whom
it was my lot to come into close contact in later years,
and neglected by the people for whom he had
laboured so long, he was laid to rest in the year
1879 in the little churchyard of his native parish of
Stranorler.

CHAPTER XII

PARTIAL FAMINE IN IRELAND—THE MANSION HOUSE COMMITTEE

1880 AND 1881

IN the spring of 1880 the Government decided upon a dissolution, to which course Mr. Gladstone had been pressing them for some time. Throughout the closing months of 1879 trade had been bad, and much distress had been felt in the mining and manufacturing districts ; whilst in Ireland, in addition to agitation for the drastic amendment of the land laws, a famine was imminent. The decision to dissolve had been kept a secret until the last moment, and was adhered to, notwithstanding the fact that two or three by-elections, notably that of Southwark, had resulted in favour of the Conservatives.

The announcement was made on March 8 by Lord Beaconsfield in the House of Lords, and by Sir Stafford Northcote in the Commons. The dissolution took place upon March 24, but before that date the manifestos of the leaders of the parties began to be issued. That of the Prime Minister took the form of a letter to the Duke of Marlborough, Lord-Lieutenant of Ireland, and expressed the hope that " all men of light and leading will resist" the destructive doctrine of the severance of the " Constitutional tie which unites it (Ireland) to Great Britain in that bond which has favoured the power and prosperity of both."

In reply, Lord Hartington disclaimed any intention of yielding to the impracticable agitation for Home Rule, and said that the agitation must be met with a firm hand, combined with the proof "that the Imperial Parliament is able and willing to grant every reasonable and just demand of the Irish people for equal laws and institutions."

Gladstone's address to the electors of Mid-Lothian contained no mention of Home Rule, nor even a promise of amendment of the land laws.

In a speech in Marylebone, Gladstone expressed the wish that the result would be decisive in favour of one party or the other ; and the result was a majority for the Liberals beyond their wildest dreams. In the words of the historian of " Our Own Times ": " With the very first day of the elections it was evident that the Conservative majority was already gone. Each succeeding day showed more and more the change that had taken place in public feeling. Defeat was turned into disaster. Disaster became utter rout and con-

fusion." When the returns of the New Parliament
were completed, it was computed that there were
349 Liberals, 243 Conservatives, and 60 Home
Rulers.

After some delay, in which first Lord Hartington
and then Lord Granville were sent for, the Queen
commanded Gladstone to form a Ministry. He did
so, and the Ministry thus formed was backed by
the largest following a Liberal Administration had
ever received. Lord Cowper became Viceroy of
Ireland, with the Right Hon. W. E. Forster his
Chief Secretary. In the hands of the latter
gentleman (who possessed a seat in the Cabinet)
was virtually vested the government of the
country.

For almost exactly two years these two well-
intentioned statesmen endeavoured to create that
friendship between the two countries which had
been the effort and disappointed hope of many of
their notable predecessors. They came to Ireland
in the hope of governing by the ordinary law of the
land, and of alleviating the country's dire distress.
They strove to ameliorate her land laws, to restrain
the harshness of some of her landlords, and to quell
the excesses of her political demagogues. They left
her in the throes of the Coercion struggle, riven
with hate between class and class, and on the eve of
a national disaster (the Park murders).

Mr. Forster's sympathetic biographer, who gives
us much information as to the events of the times,

is at pains to impress upon us that "the popular idea that he sought for this particular post is unfounded." This we may well believe, for a man who had done so much to settle the education question in England was entitled to higher office. "He took it in the spirit of the soldier who is sent to the front by his chief," and "he was not without hope that he might be able to do something towards solving that great problem of the reconciliation of the Irish people to English rule which had so long baffled the efforts of statesmanship." "Distress and disaffection—these were the two symptoms of the Irish disease. What were its causes, and how was it to be treated?" These were the problems to which Mr. Forster applied himself.

Parliament met on April 29, and the first message of good-will from the new House to the Irish people was contained in an intimation in the Queen's Speech that the Peace Preservation Act, provision for the renewal of which had not been made by the last Parliament, would not be renewed. "The Peace Preservation Act for Ireland expires with the 1st of June. You will not be asked to renew it. My desire to avoid the evils of exceptional legislation in abridgment of liberty would not induce me to forego in any degree the first duty of every Government in providing for the security of life and property. But, while determined to fulfil this sacred obligation, I am persuaded that the loyalty and good sense of my Irish subjects

will justify me in relying on the provisions of the
ordinary law, firmly administered, for the mainten-
ance of peace and order."

"The provisions enacted before the dissolution of
the last Parliament for the mitigation of distress
in Ireland have been serviceable for that important
end. The question of the sufficiency of the advances
already authorized by Parliament is under my consideration."

These amicable expressions of intention were re-
iterated in the House of Lords by Earl Spencer,
who, in reply to the Duke of Marlborough, stated
that he thought that the ordinary law of the
land would be sufficient for the government of
Ireland.

Meanwhile, on April 30, Parnell, at a meeting
in the Rotunda, made his famous "bread and lead"
speech :

> "The Americans sent me back with this
> message—that for the future you must not
> expect one cent for charity, but millions to
> break the land system. And now before I
> go I will tell you a little incident that hap-
> pened at one of our League Meetings in
> America. A gentleman came on the platform
> and handed me £25, and said, 'Here's £5 for
> bread and £20 for lead.'"

The tenor of the address was that, owing to the
impending evictions, the land question was the

burning question of the hour, but Home Rule was not to be lost sight of.

Early in the Session the Irish Party attacked the Government for not bringing in a Land Bill, and then demanded a temporary measure to avert the impending evictions. In the course of the debate Mr. Forster said he would give a considerate hearing to any proposal the Irish members wished to make. They were not slow to take advantage of this promise, and Mr. O'Connor Power introduced a short Bill which had for its object the abolition of the hanging gale which prevented tenants from taking full advantage of the Act of 1870. On June 4 Mr. Forster intimated, on the second reading, that "he was not prepared to oppose its principle," but asked time to consider the Bill.

Shortly afterwards, on June 25, Mr. Forster introduced the Compensation for Disturbance Bill, which was read a third time, but was rejected by the Lords, after two nights' debate, by 282 to 51, on August 2. Mr. Forster was very indignant at its rejection, and foresaw the extreme gravity of the situation engendered by its rejection in Ireland. Agitation commenced afresh, and day by day the country was shocked by horrible outrages. Riots and serious disturbances occurred at evictions, and a huge police force and a large body of troops had to be requisitioned to enforce the law of the land. Anyone who, in the face of his neighbourhood, dared to take an evicted farm was subjected to outrage in various forms.   Attempts on life were made, houses and stacks burned, and cattle maimed or slaughtered.

Speaking of the land laws of Ireland, let me add a word on the great topic land legislation, which in the course of a generation has transformed the face of rural Ireland.   No man has seen the results of its working more strikingly than I have; no one appreciates more clearly the present proud position of the Irish farmer, helped and petted as he has been in a variety of ways by the State.

The Act of 1870, introducing many provisions in the tenant's interests, including the right to compensation for improvements and disturbance, might be described as the start of this remarkable revolution.   Then follows the Act of 1881, establishing the Land Commission, and successively the great Purchase Acts of 1885, 1896, and 1903.

Though the treatment of the Irish tenantry by these landlords in the pre-Land Act days was in the majority of cases just and reasonable, the hard and rapacious action of a considerable minority, it is feared, attached a stigma to the whole class.   As often occurs, the good suffered for the sins of the bad, and legislation hit at landlordism altogether as a thing of sinister repute.

Previous to the Acts of 1870 and 1881, and notably the former, the lot of many Irish tenant-farmers was indeed a hard one.   They were "Between the Devil and the deep blue sea."   Many of the landlord class looked upon their tenants as simply rent-producing machines. If the tenant by the exercise of ordinary care, thrift, and labour, found himself unable to pay the exorbitant rent demanded, eviction surely followed. On the other hand, should he endeavour to improve the rent-producing power of his farm, that rent, under threat of eviction, increased in proportion to his efforts. Agitation within the law against such a system was in my opinion more than justified.

I remember during the sixties frequently appearing at Quarter Sessions for tenants served with ejectments, grounded on either the non-payment of rent or the service of a notice to quit. Of course, under the then existing law, I had no legal defence whatever, and all I could do for them was to interview the landlord or agent, and by an *ad misericordiam* appeal make the best terms I could for my unfortunate clients, and even if I did obtain some reduction in the rent demanded, the rent so reduced was a rack-rent, and so treated in after years by the Land Commission.

I have always considered that landlords would have been able to make a much stronger case, and one with better results, if, at the passing of the Act of 1870 and subsequent Acts, they had met the Government half-way, and not opposed the measures "tooth and nail." The upsetting of contracts was new to the English voter.

I have said the unhappy position of many tenants prior to the Acts of 1870 and 1881 more than justified agitation confined within the law, but it must be remembered, that agitation was against a system. The agitation of later years has been very different; it was altogether a personal one, and against individuals who were charged with disobeying laws made by themselves, and took the form of boycotting, cattle-driving, malicious fires, and other injuries to property.

Prior to the winter of 1879-80, there had been in Ireland several very bad harvests. In that winter there was an almost total failure of the potato and other crops, with the result that in very many parts of Ireland starvation was imminent, staring many of the unfortunate farmers and labourers in the face, as in the case of the famine resulting from the failure of the crops in the years 1845 to 1847. The Government were tardy in recognizing the danger, nor did the English people seem to appreciate the wretched plight in which stood a very considerable portion of the Irish population; and it was not until there appeared in the columns of *The Times* of December 16, an appeal from Her Grace the Duchess of Marlborough, asking the English nation to contribute funds towards relieving the terrible distress then existing in Ireland, that they awoke to the fact that unless help came there would be a bad famine in Ireland. The committee formed by Her Grace were able to relieve some of the distress, as the funds collected amounted to over £60,000.

But towards the close of the year 1879, it was known in Dublin that the funds collected by Her Grace in England, though large in amount, would not nearly be sufficient to meet the great emergency, and accordingly the Lord Mayor called a meeting of the citizens at the Mansion House, which was attended by persons of all shades of politics and religious beliefs. The meeting stood adjourned till January 2, 1880, to enable Mr. Edmund Dwyer Gray, M.P., who was the incoming Lord Mayor, to preside, and on that day a committee was formed, including most, if not all, of the principal citizens of Dublin, of every class, religion, and politics.

It is not my intention to write here at any length as to the immense amount of work done by the Dublin Mansion House Committee. The full report of its action and results has been written for the committee by Mr. William O'Brien, M.P.

At a meeting of January 2, 1880, Sir Arthur Guinness, M.P. (the late Lord Ardilaun) proposed, and Mr. P. J. Smyth, M.P., seconded, a resolution calling the attention of the world to the dire calamity threatening the peasantry of our country. There was an immediate and general response from all parts of the world. Subscriptions flowed in; Australia, North and South America, Canada, India, France, and England—all contributed, and the amount received by the committee totalled over £181,000, as against over £86,000 received by a somewhat similar committee during the bad times of 1847. The distribution of that large sum of money was an immense undertaking, but it was cheerfully performed by the Executive Committee. To cope with the amount to be done, some of us had to work the greater part of the day, and frequently to a late hour at night.

I think it right here, and not out of place, to insert the names of the Executive Committee. They were the following :

The Lord Mayor (Edmund Dwyer Gray, M.P.), Alderman Tarpey, Rev. Canon Bagot, C. J. Bridgett, David Drummond, Colonel Davoren, V. B. Dillon, junior, George Delaney, Very Rev. James Daniel, P.P., David Drimmie, William Lane Joynt, Charles Kennedy, J. F. Lombard, George Sigerson, M.D., Maurice Brooks, M.P., J. A. Fox, T. Maxwell Hutton, Alderman Harris, William M. Murphy, Sir James Mackey, Sir George B. Owens, Thomas Pim, P. J. Smyth, M.P., P. McCabe Fay, Lord F. Godolphin Osborne, Jonathan Pim, John Wallis, Richard Allen, Sir John Barrington, the Hon. David R. Plunkett, Most Rev. Dr. Trench (Protestant Archbishop of Dublin), with Mr. J. H. Wright as assistant-secretary.

I am grieved to add that very few of the Executive Committee still survive. Among the survivors I am glad to find my valued friend Dr. George Sigerson (now a member of the Senate of the National University), who did yeoman's service on the committee. Day and night saw him working; he was indefatigable in his anxiety to help the impoverished, and in some districts fever-stricken, people. His report, made by him in conjunction with the late Dr. J. C. Kenny, on the fever-stricken districts of Mayo, all of which they visited, was of great value and assistance to the committee.

I had the charge of the correspondence other than routine; it was a very difficult task. Local sub-committees had to be formed, and their applications considered and replied to. One of the rules of our committee was that each sub-committee should have as members the Protestant rector and the parish priest. In the vast proportion of cases there was no difficulty, all working smoothly and harmoniously.

The late Archbishop Trench was a most kindly and lovable gentleman, and was a constant attendant at our meetings. It was altogether due to his friendly advice and wisdom that during the entire time the committee was in existence no single division took place. In conducting my correspondence I had frequently to consult His Grace, and I always found him strictly impartial and just. On one occasion I found a sub-committee had neither the parish priest nor the rector as members. The parish priest would not act with the rector, and the latter returned the compliment. I consulted the Archbishop as to what was the best course to adopt. The poor people were starving and badly needed a cheque, which, under the rule, I could not send them. He advised me to send a cheque in the names of the two gentlemen, with directions to the secretary that it was not to be used unless signed by both clergymen in each other's presence in the committee-room. The result of His Grace's advice was, as we expected, that the two payees in the cheque, rather than deprive the poor people of their grant, came together, were introduced, and became fast friends.

Except in one instance, I found all the sub-committees, both Protestant and Catholic, worked most harmoniously. In one case we had sent to a convent in the west as much as we thought they were entitled to, and I wrote to the reverend mother to that effect. One morning shortly afterwards I was told in the Mansion House that a clergyman wanted to see me. On going out to the hall, I met a young parson, who informed me he had come as a deputation from the convent, asking for an additional cheque. Under the circumstances I could not refuse him, and he returned home with a cheque for the nuns in his pocket. I was aware that great poverty did prevail in the district, but the funds were running short.

The leaders of the Land League, apparently, did not trust the composition of the committee, though on it were the two Archbishops of Dublin and the

Bishops of Ireland ; and accordingly Mr. Parnell
and Mr. Dillon opened a crusade against it in
America, insisting that all funds should be entrusted
to the Land League, to be distributed by that
body.

We were, however, able to reply to their criti-
cisms day by day. Thanks to the kindness of
the Anglo-American Telegraph Company and the
Eastern Extension Company, which allowed us free
telegraphic communication with America, Australia,
and India, the charges levelled at the action and
formation of the committee by these gentlemen,
appearing in the American press, had their answer
in the morning papers—if not, next day.

Of the total sum of over £181,000 received by
the committee, Asia contributed over £20,000 ;
Africa contributed £1,407 ; America, Canada, New-
foundland, La Plata, British Guiana, and Mauritius,
contributed between them £26,875 ; Australasia
contributed £94,916.

Outside the United Kingdom the only nation in
Europe which came to the relief of the starving
Irish peasantry was France, which country, bur-
dened as she had been, and was, by the heavy
impost placed on her by Germany as a result of
the Franco-German War, nevertheless sent the
magnificent contribution of over 700,000 francs—
£28,000.

The rule that clergymen of both religions should
be on the sub-committee was only broken in three

cases. These were cases in which the Protestant clergyman was an agent of the Irish Church Missions; and, as some of the parishioners of the Missions were in admittedly great poverty, on the advice of Dr. Trench a separate grant was made to each, with the intimation that any attempt at proselytism would result in grants being stopped.

In only one case, referred to farther on, was any charge of unfair dealing brought against the committee. It came from Kilronan, Arran Island, and was brought by the Protestant rector of the place, the Rev. William Kilbride, representative of the Irish Church Missions, and by Mr. Thomas H. Thompson, agent to the owner of the island. The allegation was that these two gentlemen had been improperly kept off the sub-committee, and that some of the destitute poor had been improperly refused relief, because they had worked for them. As the charges had been openly made, and constituted the first and only case in which improper action had been charged against one of our sub-committees, at the suggestion of the late Mr. Charles Kennedy, who was a most active member of the committee, and with the concurrence of the Most Rev. Dr. Trench, I determined to go down to the Island, and personally and on the spot investigate the charges. Accordingly, on June 19, 1880, I proceeded to Aranmore, crossing from Galway in a "hooker"—a large, roomy sailing-boat.

I wrote to all the parties interested, and finally fixed Monday, June 21, to hear the objections of Mr. Thompson and Rev. W. Kilbride, both of whom attended, as also did Father Fahey, C.C., and two members of the sub-committee.

I heard all sides patiently, and thoroughly investigated the charges brought against the sub-committee, and came to the conclusion, and so reported, that the charges brought by Mr. Thompson and Rev. W. Kilbride had totally failed. No persons had been refused relief because, as alleged, they were friends of Rev. W. Kilbride, but simply because they were earning good wages under him. He was not on the committee because he had only one Protestant parishioner, and the latter was a large shopkeeper. Mr. Thompson had, when requested, refused to act on the sub-committee. On the whole I was quite satisfied that everyone on the island requiring relief had obtained it.

CHAPTER XIII

THE QUEEN *v.* PARNELL AND OTHERS—
MR. FORSTER AND THE LAND LEAGUE

ABOUT this time Mr. Forster was beginning to be shaken in his conviction that Ireland could be governed by the ordinary laws of the kingdom. On August 4, in a debate upon a Home Rule motion initiated by Parnell, he plainly intimated that, if the Government did not find its powers sufficient to enforce the law in Ireland, they would ask Parliament for further powers. Nevertheless, he was all the time hoping that the fierce lawlessness that prevailed might be adequately met by the ordinary law and the promise of a good Land Bill.

Parliament was prorogued on September 7, and immediately the Irish Members took the field against the Government. Less than a fortnight after the rising of Parliament, Mr. Parnell delivered his famous Ennis speech, in which, advising the tenants not to attend the Commission which had been appointed to inquire into the land question, and throwing cold water upon the intention of the

Government to pass a Land Bill, he went on to say : " Depend upon it that the measure of the Land Bill next Session will be the measure of your activity and energy this winter. It will be the measure of your determination not to bid for farms from which others have been evicted, and to use the strong force of public opinion to deter any unjust men amongst yourselves—and there are many such— from bidding for such farms. Now, what are you to do to a tenant who bids for a farm from which his neighbour has been evicted ?" (Here there was much tumult, with cries of " Kill him ! Shoot him !")

When the noise had subsided he went on : " Now, I think I heard somebody say, ' Shoot him !' But I wish to point out a very much better way—a more Christian and charitable way, which will give the lost sinner an opportunity of repenting." He then proceeded to enunciate the famous doctrine of " boy- cotting." " When a man takes a farm from which another man has been evicted, you must show him on the roadside when you meet him, you must show him in the streets of the town, you must show him at the shop counter, you must show him at the fair, and in the market-place, and even in the house of worship, by leaving him severely alone, by putting him in a moral Coventry, by isolating him from his kind as if he were a leper of old—you must show him your detestation of the crime he has committed ; and you may depend upon it that there will be no man so full of avarice, so lost to shame, as to dare the public opinion of all right-thinking men, and to transgress your unwritten code of laws."

Right loyally did the peasantry act upon the advice of their leaders. Their resistance to process-servers who were serving processes on the Erne estate at the instance of Captain Boycott, the agent, and the subsequent intimidation of his neighbours and servants from gathering his crops, gave this mode of dealing with a political enemy or other obnoxious person the name of the man to whom it first applied.

The Land League had by this time constituted courts of its own, and it enforced its decrees by the most merciless and ruthless boycotting, and all sorts of agrarian outrages. On September 25 Lord Mountmorres, a landlord who had much trouble with tenantry, was murdered near his own residence, Ebor, County Galway, and a profound sensation was caused throughout the United Kingdom. Loud was the demand in the press and on public platforms for coercive measures to be at once introduced. Mr. Forster was now being driven, in spite of all his hopes and all his good intentions towards Ireland, first to request a re-institution of those coercive measures which he hated and loathed. To this request was added a threat on his part to resign if the request was not granted. No more pathetic reading can be found in the life of any statesman, or illuminative of the state of mind of a man of principle being driven to act against his principles, than his correspondence with his chief in the autumn of 1880. Even whilst demanding repressive legislation, he never fails to keep to the front remedial measures.

On October 9, in his speech at the banquet to the Ministers at the Guildhall, Gladstone said that the time had not yet come for extra measures. But on the 23rd the Cabinet decided to prosecute Parnell and others for conspiracy. Meanwhile Forster agreed not to ask Gladstone to summon Parliament until early in January.

The trial of the Queen *v.* Parnell and others commenced on Tuesday, December 28, 1880, and terminated on Tuesday, January 25, 1881, in the disagreement of the jury. The Court at first consisted of the Lord Chief Justice May, Mr. Justice (afterwards Lord) Fitzgerald, and Mr. Justice (afterwards Lord Justice) Barry.

The names of the traversers were: Charles Stewart Parnell, John Dillon, Joseph Gillis Bigger, Timothy Daniel Sullivan, Thomas Sexton, Patrick Egan, Thomas Brennan, Michael M. O'Sullivan, Michael P. Boyton, Patrick Joseph Sheridan, Patrick Joseph Gordon, Mathew Harris, John W. Walsh, and John W. Nally.

The Crown was represented by the Right Hon. Hugh Law, M.P., Attorney - General; William Moore Johnson, M.P., Solicitor-General; Denis

Caulfield Heron, Third Sergeant; James Murphy, Q.C.; Andrew Marshall Porter, Q.C.; John Naish, Q.C., Law Adviser; Constantine Molloy, and David Ross—instructed by William Lane Joynt, D.L., Crown and Treasury Solicitor. Mr. Macdonough, Q.C., led for the defence, instructed by Mr. Valentine B. Dillon, junior, and the names of the other counsel for the traversers were: Samuel Walker, Q.C., William McLaughlin, Q.C., Peter O'Brien, Q.C., John Adye Curran, Francis Nolan, Luke Dillon, Richard Adams, and A. M. Sullivan.

In arranging as to the amount of the refresher fees, Valentine Dillon told me he intended giving ten guineas to each of the junior counsel, with a stipulation that they should give their entire time to the case. I personally refused to give up the entire of my time for that amount, and, as Mr. Parnell wished particularly to have the benefit of my services, Mr. Dillon consented to give me fifteen guineas per day, this being five guineas more than was paid to the other juniors. It is needless to add that our leader, Mr. Macdonough, insisted on a consultation every evening.

Previous to the case being called a somewhat extraordinary incident took place. The Lord Chief Justice, referring to some severe strictures passed on him for certain observations made by him on a former occasion, in delivering judgment in an application to postpone the trial, said he denied that he had imputed guilt to the traversers, but as the Chief Magistrate he did what he considered his duty in referring to the very disordered state of the country. His lordship denied positively that he was conscious of any favour between the Crown and the traversers, and added that he felt he should deal with the entire case with that impartiality which is the first duty of a Judge. Still, it had suggested itself to him that, in the present trial, considering the critical state of this country, it was most important to remove every element that might tend to disturb the calm and dispassionate consideration of the case. He concluded by saying : "Upon the whole, after anxious consideration and with the concurrence of some whose opinions I highly value, I have come to the conclusion that the due administration of justice will be promoted by my not taking part in the hearing of the case." After some further observations his lordship withdrew.

The indictment against the traversers contained nineteen counts, and averred generally that they were guilty of a conspiracy in inciting tenants not to pay rents contracted for, and deterring tenants by various forms of boycotting from payment of rents, or the taking of evicted farms.

The nineteenth and last count was the cause of a lengthened discussion, and involved the sudden shortening of the trial. It was proposed and insisted on by Mr. Macdonough, Q.C., that we were entitled under its wording to give evidence as to the impoverished state of the country, and the extent to which evictions were a contributing cause of misery. The count ran as follows : " That the defendants did among themselves wickedly and seditiously conspire to cause and create discontent and disaffection among the liege subjects of Her Majesty, and to promote and excite feelings of ill-will and hostility between different classes of Her Majesty's subjects." We had brought up witnesses from different parts of Ireland to give evidence as to the number of evictions, and their results to the impoverished tenants—in death, the poorhouse, and emigration.

An old man named Berry, eighty-three years of age, was put into the witness-box, and stated he was then in the poorhouse, that in 1847 he was a tenant under Lord Lucan in the county Mayo.

" How many people did you yourself see put out in the year 1848 ?" was asked ; but this question was objected to by the Attorney-General as being irrelevant. Mr. Macdonough contended it was open to him, under the general words of the nineteenth count, to put the question and have it answered. The Court agreed with this argument, with the result that the Crown at once entered a *nolle prosequi* on that count.

CHAPTER XIV

INCIDENTS OF THE PARNELL TRIAL—
MR. MACDONOUGH

FRANCIS MACDONOUGH, Q.C., was a born leader
in *nisi prius* and jury cases. He never showed
his power more than when he conducted the case
of the Queen *v.* Parnell and others. There were
eight counsel for the defence, and he managed that
each of them should select one or more of the
defendants nominally to defend in order that all
should have an opportunity of speaking. There
were many discordant elements, temperamental as
well as political, among the counsel. I had the
honour of appearing for Mr. Matt Harris and
a man named Scrab Nally, the latter of whom
was a believer in arguments which, to use his
own picturesque phrase, were " bullets and not
talk."

In consultation, Mr. Macdonough suggested that
it would be better to refer in the speeches as little
as possible, if at all, to the facts of the case. He
eventually gave leave to all the counsel except two
to speak from any political point of view they

might select. The excepted two he told to make
the best case they could upon the evidence. I was
one of the two. My colleague afterwards told me
he would not follow Mr. Macdonough's suggestion,
and so in the end I was the only one left to speak
to the facts.

It was late in the afternoon when my turn to
speak came on. I knew very well that I had a
splendid case to speak to, but Mr. Macdonough,
who shared with the other counsel the anxiety to
avoid the facts, told me before I commenced to be
very short and certainly to conclude that evening.
After I had been talking for about an hour and a
half, to my astonishment Mr. Macdonough stood
up and suggested that the Court should adjourn,
as it would be unfair for me to speak any more
that evening. Judge (afterwards Lord) Fitzgerald
asked me, if he adjourned, how long I should take in
the morning. I replied half an hour. That evening, at consultation, Mr. Macdonough was very
angry that I had confined myself to half an hour,
and said he should insist upon my going on for a
much longer time. This I refused to do, being
unwilling to break my word to the Judge, and
reminded him that he had told me to speak only
for a short time. His answer was, that he had no
idea I should have made so good a case upon the
facts. I kept my word to the Judge next morning.
I was told afterwards that I had brought over three
wavering jurors.

The jury in the case had been selected under what was called the Old System, and the final selection took place before the Master in his office. Mr. Macdonough arranged that, as I had an intimate knowledge of the politics and religion of all the jurors, I should appear with himself before the Master, and instructed me that, as soon as Mr. Joynt, the Treasury and Crown Solicitor, had objected to three Catholics, I should call his attention openly to the fact. Accordingly, as soon as the third Catholic had been objected to, I said : " Mr. Macdonough, that is the third Catholic Mr. Joynt has ordered to stand aside !" Mr. Macdonough, who had appeared to be taking no interest in what was going on, immediately threw up his hands in a melodramatic manner, calling out :

" My God, he is striking off every Catholic !"

No more Catholic jurors were struck off, but I believe Mr. Joynt never forgave me.

Judge Fitzgerald, in the beginning of his charge to the jury, accurately diagnosed my position as counsel. After paying a well-deserved tribute of praise to the various counsel for the defence, he named each in turn in the following language : " Mr. Dillon, solicitor for the defendants, has managed to secure for his clients the veteran experience and unceasing watchfulness of Mr. Macdonough, he has secured also the simplicity and persuasive voice of Mr. Walker, and I may say also the vigorous and honest outcome of Mr. McLaughlin, the fiery zeal and unpurchasable eloquence of one whom I will call the descendant of O'Brien Boroihme. He has had also the historic lore of Nolan, the portly presence and polished wit of Mr. Luke Dillon, and also the genius of Adams and of Sullivan, and I say unfeignedly of these two last gentlemen—that is, of Mr. Adams and Mr. Sullivan —I can only say in one sentence, that they have amply proved in this trial their right henceforth to take their places amongst the first forensic advocates of the day. You will observe that from this category I have omitted the name of my friend, John Adye Curran, but it is to give him the greatest praise of all, for although we have listened to wonderful and eloquent speeches—certainly not too long—I give to Mr. Curran the praise of being the only one who has spoken really to the issues of the trial. And indeed, with naive simplicity, he told us that at a consultation—and I can fancy myself present—he was told by his leader that somebody must speak to the issues, and that that duty was placed upon him."

I may add that I am the sole survivor of the above-named counsel for the defence.

During the course of the trial, there were several dinners given to Mr. Parnell and such of the other traversers as could be present. I gave one, and Valentine B. Dillon gave another. At my party there were present (with the exception of Mr.

Macdonough, Q.C.) all the counsel engaged in the case, including Samuel Walker, Q.C., William McLaughlin, Q.C., Peter O'Brien, Q.C., and A. M. Sullivan. The traversers present included Charles Stewart Parnell, John Dillon, Mr. Bigger, Patrick Egan, and many others. I am not quite sure if Michael Davitt was one of the company, but I know he was present at one of the parties. I entrusted the menu to a friendly neighbour, Mr. Edward O. MacDevitt, who was well up in such matters. The company was the same at the two dinners. Viewed in the light of after years it was a strange company, and one not likely again to be brought together. Mr. Samuel Walker also gave a dinner to Mr. Parnell at which ladies were present.

The late George Keys, formerly Divisional Justice in Dublin, told me a very good story of Mr. Macdonough. They both were engaged to defend District Inspector Montgomery, charged with the murder of a bank manager in a northern county. The jury disagreed on the first trial, and after they had been discharged, he turned to Keys, saying: "My dear young friend, you have saved that man's life." Keys, thinking Mr. Macdonough referred to his speech for the defence, of course replied that he was greatly pleased and flattered at the compliment. "Yes," continued Mr. Macdonough, "you saved his life by advising that I should be brought down to defend him." Alas, poor Keys!

On another occasion Mr. Macdonough was en-

gaged to defend a gentleman charged with a very
serious offence.   His fee, as arranged with the
solicitor, was one hundred guineas, plus consultation
fee and twenty-five guineas refresher.   The present
Judge Boyd and I were briefed with him.   The
case for the Crown concluded on the first day.
When we met in court next morning, there was no
Mr. Macdonough.   Neither Judge Boyd nor I was
prepared to state the case without some preparation, and we informed the Judge that we understood from Mr. Macdonough the previous evening
that he certainly would attend.

The presiding Judge adjourned for a short period,
and our solicitor went down to the Library, only to
return with a message from Mr. Macdonough to
the effect that he had too many cases to attend
to, and could not possibly come to Green Street.
Our client was then sent to look him up, and returned shortly afterwards with him.   He had to
pay a second hundred guineas before he consented
to come.   Happily the traverser was acquitted,
so I suppose the client considered the money well
spent.

CHAPTER XV

MR. FORSTER'S TROUBLED PATH

On January 7, 1881, the Session of Parliament began, and the Queen's Speech contained the following passage: "I grieve to state that the social condition of Ireland has assumed an alarming character. Agrarian crimes in general have multiplied far beyond the experience of recent years. Attempts upon life have not grown in the same proportion as other offences, but I must add that applications have been made for personal protection far beyond all former precedent by the police under the supervision of the Executive. I have to notice other evils yet more widely spread; the administration of justice has been frustrated with respect to these offences through the impossibility of procuring evidence, and an extended system of terror has thus been established in various parts of the country which has paralyzed alike the exercise of private rights and the performance of civil duties. In a state of things new in some important respects,

114

and hence with little available guidance from former precedent, I have deemed it right, steadily to put into use the ordinary powers of the law before making any new demand.   But a demonstration of their insufficiency, amply supplied by the present circumstances, leads me to apprise you that proposals will be immediately submitted to you for entrusting me with additional powers, necessary, in my judgment, not only for vindication of order and public law, but likewise to secure, on behalf of my subjects, protection for life and property."

In consequence Forster gave notice that he would move for leave to bring in a Bill for the better protection of person and property, and to amend drastically the law relating to the possession of arms.   His repugnance to the task he explained in the close of a speech explaining the provisions of the Bill: "This has been to me a most painful duty.   I never expected that I should have to discharge it.   If I had thought that this duty would devolve on the Irish Secretary, I would never have held the office.   If I could have seen that this would be the result of twenty years of Parliamentary life, I would have left Parliament rather than have undertaken it."

The Bill was introduced on January 24, and its passage through Parliament was impeded by the furious and persistent obstruction of the Irish members, which gave rise to the closure rules of the following year. On one occasion the House of Commons sat for forty-one and a half consecutive hours, from a Monday afternoon to a Wednesday morning, when the Speaker took the matter in his own hands and put the question. Finally the whole of Parnell's followers were suspended from the service of the House, and the Bill, accelerated, became law on March 2. I refer hereafter to this Act as the Coercion Act of 1881.

Conciliation, however, came close upon the heels of Coercion, and on April 7 Mr. Gladstone introduced a revolutionary Land Bill, embodying the Report of the Bessborough Commission in favour of not only fair rents, but fixity of tenure and free sale—the "three F's," as they were afterwards called. On July 3 the Bill was read a third time by 220 to 14, and on August 22 became law. Its passage was an almost incredible legislative feat. No party was enthusiastic for its success. "The Whigs were disaffected about it, the Radicals doubted it; the Tories thought that property as a principal was ruined by it; the Irishmen, when the humour seized them, bade him send the Bill to line trunks" (Lord Morley).

The Act was received with reserve and suspicion by the Irish leaders. After two large Land League Conventions, one held in Dublin on September 14

and another held in Maryborough on the 26th of
the same month, it was decided to select cases to
be tried by the newly constituted Land Courts.
The test cases were not to be cases of extreme
hardship, but cases in which the rent had not
hitherto been considered exorbitant ; and, pending
their decision, no member of the League was to
apply to have a fair rent fixed without the consent
of the local branch.

Mr. Forster now came to the conclusion that it
was the intention of Parnell and his followers to
balk and render of no effect all the efforts of
British statesmen to solve the Irish problem, and
accordingly he suggested to Mr. Gladstone to
denounce Parnell's policy in a speech which he
was to make in Leeds on October 7.   This Mr.
Gladstone did in no uncertain language, and
reminding his audience in a memorable phrase
that the "resources of civilization were not yet
exhausted."   Parnell replied in Wexford in a
speech on October 9, conveying veiled taunts to
the Ministers to do their worst.   On Wednesday,
the 12th, the Cabinet decided to send Parnell to
prison under the Coercion Act of 1881, which had
just been passed, and the next day he was arrested
and lodged in Kilmainham.

On October 17 the " No Rent " manifesto, calling
upon all tenants to abstain from paying rents until
the constitutional rights of the people had been

restored, was published in *United Ireland.* The manifesto met with immediate disapproval and condemnation on the part of the Catholic clergy, and even the people made no attempt to carry out its exhortations.

CHAPTER XVI

APPOINTED DIVISIONAL MAGISTRATE

FOR some years previous to the end of the year 1881 I had been overworked, and my health was not so good as I could have wished. I had a very fair practice at the Bar, but my work was very hard and heavy; I frequently had to travel by night to work in the daytime, and in the beginning of the year 1880 I often sat up to a late hour working on the Dublin Mansion House Committee, so I was glad when Lord O'Hagan offered me a silk gown, feeling that I should soon make up the temporary loss of income after a good rest—for my receipts for some years previous had been considerable. However, the fates decreed otherwise.

One night the late Richard Adams came to see me, and informed me that he had just been speaking to a friend, a Member of Parliament, who had been dining with Lord Cowper, and that His Excellency remarked, speaking of the then existing vacancy in the position of Dublin Police Magistrate, that he had heard a man named Curran mentioned for the office, but did not like to appoint him, as he

119

(Mr. Curran) had not asked for the position, and he was not previously acquainted with him. Adams told me to send in my application at once. I refused, saying that I did not covet the position, and should have to consider the matter if it was offered to me, but certainly should not ask for it.

I understood afterwards that Adams saw William Findlater, M.P., and Maurice Brooks, M.P., next morning, and that they drove out to the Viceregal Lodge and personally asked Lord Cowper to appoint me. At that time the land business in all the counties was in full working order, and I had briefs to go down in many cases. I was engaged in one of them before Romney Foley, Q.C., and Lawrence Doyle (afterwards Legal Land Commissioner), when I received a wire from my wife, saying Lord Cowper had sent to say he wished to see me that day. I wired, saying I should call next morning. At this time I had made up my mind, after consulting my wife, to accept the position, if offered.

On going into the Viceregal Lodge, I met the late Mr. Thomas H. Burke, who said to me: "I hope you are going to say 'Yes.'" When I went in before His Excellency, he shook hands and said he was very anxious to offer me the office of Police Magistrate, but felt a difficulty, as he did not even know my appearance. "Well, sir," I replied, "you will not offer me the position if you are to judge by my appearance, as no one thinks much of that except my wife."

He laughed heartily, and said he was quite satisfied with it, and offered me the position, which I accepted. I walked back to the Courts, and on my way along the quays Mr. Burke overtook me on a car, and asked me, was it all right. I replied, "Yes," and he then drove off, saying he would tell them in the Castle, and he was sure all would be pleased. I never saw him afterwards.

In the year 1881, and some time before he resigned, Lord O'Hagan sent my old friend Charles Teeling, K.C., his secretary, to me and to the late George Keys, saying he intended calling us within the Bar, if we so wished. I consented, as I had been, as stated above, lately in bad health and overworked, but he imposed one condition, that we were not to mention the matter until after the call had taken place, as at every former giving of silk a certain gentleman had gone to him insisting on his right to be included in the number. Unfortunately, George Keys confided the matter, in the strictest confidence, to a friend, with the result that it was soon known generally. Next day I was informed that the Lord Chancellor would not call either of us at that time, as our friend had heard of it, and had been insisting on being included. Lord O'Hagan told me he would leave me as a legacy to his successor. This, in fact, he did, but in the meantime I had been appointed Police Magistrate. And in the year 1882 I wrote to Lord Chancellor Law, reminding him of Lord O'Hagan's promise. In reply, the Chancellor wrote, saying it was most unusual to give a man a silk gown after he had ceased being a practising barrister, but having regard to Lord O'Hagan's wishes, and to the fact that I had been appointed before they could be carried out, he would take upon himself to break the rules.

I was all the better pleased to receive the honour at his hands, because I had come to know and appreciate him during the long trial of the Queen *v.* Moore, to which I have already referred.

The Dublin Metropolitan Police Magistrates are not supposed to be called on to take charge of the military in aid of the civil power. However, I had to do so once during my brief tenure of office as Divisional Justice. It was on the occasion of the strike of the Dublin Metropolitan Police Force. It is not my intention here to discuss their alleged grievance, whether real or otherwise; suffice it to say, it was a time of great anxiety and peril in Dublin and district. The preservation of peace and enforcing of law had to be entrusted to a number of special constables, who were private citizens. One gentleman I remember as having been sworn in by me was Mr. Richard J. Barry, who now so efficiently discharges the duties of Crown Solicitor for the King's County.

By direction of the Lord-Lieutenant I was told to take charge of Kingstown and surrounding districts. Early in the day I saw there was a bad and disorderly crowd in the town, and I considered it my duty to make an order to have all public-houses closed at six o'clock. There was, however, a difficulty in communicating with each, and writing out the necessary order to be served. A number of strikers were lounging about the office, and I explained to them what I wanted. I was well known to them all, some of them being old members of the force, and I asked them, as a favour to myself, would they write out and serve the notices for me. Their unanimous reply was, "We will"; and so they did. During the course of the day I received a letter from the Castle stating that by His Excellency's order a company of soldiers was being sent to Kingstown to aid the Civil Power, and that they were to be under my orders as magistrate. The letter requested me to take charge of them. Shortly afterwards they arrived, and I asked the officer in command to keep them confined to the Town Hall pending orders from me.

It was then after six o'clock, and as the supply of whisky had suddenly run short, the disorder in the street consisted mainly of horseplay and shouting and booing, so I considered that the presence of the military on the street would only infuriate these half-drunken men and lead to an attack on the soldiers.

While I was in the Police-Office a sergeant hurriedly entered and said there was bad work going on about the Town Hall, and that it was likely to be worse, as the soldiers had been all drawn up along the street. I hurried up and asked the officer in command whom I had previously interviewed by whose authority the men had been paraded. At this moment a rather pompous-looking officer came up and said it was by his order. I told him what I thought of his order, and said that a very serious riot would be the result. Then a lucky thought struck me; I asked him by what authority he had given the order. He replied, by the authority of the Castle, where he had been sworn in as a magistrate. In reply to my question, Had he any written authority? he said he did not want it.

"Oh yes, you do," I answered, producing the written order from His Excellency to me to take charge. I then informed him that he would disobey my order at his peril, and that my order was that the soldiers should at once be sent back to the Town Hall. I had the satisfaction of seeing my order carried out, and as a result the disorderly conduct gradually subsided, and Kingstown resumed its normal state.

There was at one time a very ruffianly element
to the fore in James's Street, Dublin. So bad was
it that it became almost as much as a constable's
life was worth to attempt to arrest one of the gang.
While I was acting as magistrate a fine young
constable appeared before me charging six men
with having been members of a mob which had
brutally attacked him, and beaten and kicked him
while on the ground. (This constable, whose name
was Cox, was afterwards shot in Middle Abbey
Street while engaged in quelling a disturbance in
that street between rival factions of the Fenian
body.) He appeared before me with his head all
bandaged, and stated that after he had arrested a
prisoner for some offence, he was surrounded by
a mob, knocked down, and badly kicked. In reply
to the solicitor for prisoners, he stated that none
of the prisoners struck him, but they were in the
crowd, shouting, cheering, and booing. I was then
asked by the solicitor to discharge his clients, as
they had not been identified as having struck the
constable. I refused, stating that it was well that
the gentlemen of James's Street should understand
the law, which made anyone acting as they had
done equally guilty with the principals. I then
sentenced each to six months' imprisonment. After
that matters quieted down very quickly in James's
Street. A constable could arrest a prisoner with
perfect safety ; the friends, in place of trying to

help him, separated in all directions, fearing to come within my rule of being treated as " aiders and abettors." The law on the subject they seemed quite to understand.

CHAPTER XVII

THE DARK DAYS OF THE EARLY EIGHTIES

THE history of the year 1882—the centenary anniversary of Parliamentary Independence of Ireland—might well be written in blood. The record of every month is stained with atrocious outrage, deplored by the adherents of the National party as fatal to its cause, and pointed to by the opponents of that party as a convincing demonstration of the utterly lawless spirit of the Irish people.

Coercion had failed, notwithstanding the fact that hundreds of "suspects" were in gaol at the beginning of the year under the Coercion Act of 1881, and that three of the leaders (Parnell, Dillon, and O'Kelly) were safely lodged in Kilmainham Prison. There was, it is true, some slight diminution in crime during the month of January, but, as the year wore on, the passage in the Queen's Speech at the opening of Parliament on February 7—"The condition of Ireland shows signs of improvement" —was entirely belied, and when the tale of the year came to be told, it was found that there were twenty-six murders against a total of twenty-five for the previous two years 1880 and 1881, and an increase of 297 offences above the average of those two years.

Conciliation, in the form of the Land Act, too, had failed, and the Cabinet was becoming divided as to which policy was to be pursued. The difficulty of renewing the Peace Preservation Act was very great. The closure rules introduced by Mr. Gladstone on February 14, which were bitterly resisted by both Tory and Irish members, had not yet been passed, and much valuable time might be wasted in pushing a new Crimes Act through Parliament if the Irish members adopted the obstructive tactics of a former occasion. The Ministry itself might be imperilled. On the other hand, if the Government allowed the Act to lapse in spite of the representations of the Irish Secretary, the suspects would have to be released and the Executive would have again to rely upon the ordinary law of the land to preserve order in Ireland.

In March the suspects in prison amounted to 872 persons, and on the 25th of that month Forster, referring to the pressure from within and without the Cabinet in favour of the abandonment of coercion, says in a letter to Gladstone : " Ireland will certainly be ungovernable if we give up the Protection Act without replacing it by other strong measures." In the House of Commons, on March 29, Forster threatened sterner measures, and some of his colleagues resented what they conceived to be an intimation that these measures had the consideration and approval of the Cabinet.

Meanwhile the House of Lords had appointed a Select Committee to inquire into the working of the Land Act, which had been in operation only about four months; and this provoked from Gladstone a motion on March 10 in these terms: "That in the opinion of this House a Parliamentary inquiry into the working of the Irish Land Act must defeat the operation of that Act, and be injurious in its effects upon the good government of Ireland." The inquiry was afterwards dropped. The growing antagonism of the public, and the opposition of his colleagues to a continuance of the coercion policy, and some articles in the *Pall Mall*, caused Forster to write to Gladstone on April 4 as follows: "I seize, however, this opportunity of saying to you what has been in my mind for some time—that if now, or at any future time, you think that from any cause it would be to the public service or for the good of Ireland that I should resign, I most unreservedly place my resignation in your hands." To this Gladstone replied that if Forster resigned upon the Irish question he (Gladstone) would have to go too.

Agrarian outrage of the graver kind, murder, manslaughter, and firing at the person, had greatly increased in number for the last quarter of 1881 and the first quarter of 1882, and in a letter of April 7, to Gladstone, Mr. Forster outlined the manner in which the powers of the Executive should be strengthened under the new Crimes Act. One of his suggestions was the suspension of trial by jury.

An event now happened which brought Mr. Gladstone and the other members of the Cabinet who had supported Forster to set their faces against a new Crimes Act. On April 10 Parnell was released on parole, to enable him to go to Paris to attend the funeral of his niece. In the course of his journey Parnell met Captain O'Shea, and repeated to him a conversation he had with Mr. Justin McCarthy the day before as to the possibility of peace in Ireland if a satisfactory Arrears Bill was passed. O'Shea communicated this to Gladstone and Chamberlain, who were much impressed. Parnell, upon his return to Kilmainham, wrote a letter on April 28, upon the same lines, to O'Shea, which O'Shea showed to Forster. Forster sent the letter to Gladstone, and also an account of his interview with O'Shea, and the result was that on May.2 Gladstone wired Lord Cowper to release Parnell, Dillon, and O'Kelly. Before the order for release was signed Cowper resigned, and, on the advice of Forster, Lord Spencer, who had previously been Viceroy, was appointed in his place. The resignation of Mr. Forster followed.

CHAPTER XVIII

THE TRAGEDY OF MAY 6, 1882

THE treaty was made. An Arrears Bill and the relaxation of coercion was the price of the "uncrowned" king's discouragement of the more violent agitation. For English administration it was peace at any price; for Parnell and his followers it was peace with honour, and the peace of victory.

Change of policy meant change of administrators, and in the end of April Lord-Lieutenant Cowper and his Chief Secretary, Mr. Forster, made way for Earl Spencer and Lord Frederick Cavendish—Ireland's governors under the "new régime." In Ireland Lord Spencer was at least well known. He had been Viceroy in the Government of Mr. Gladstone 1868-1874, and had well proved his capacity and statesmanship. Lord Frederick Cavendish, was little more than a name. But it was a distinguished name, for he was a scion of a great house, a son of the Duke of Devonshire, and was known to be a man of high character and generous nature, and any lack of attainments or qualifications for the great office were expected

131

to be most amply made up for by a most anxious and genuine desire to pacificate Ireland. A policy of amelioration and conciliation requires more than a well-disposed administrator. At times it may require the resolution of a tyrannical dictator, and, partly obscured by the dignities of the Viceregal office, Lord Frederick Cavendish had behind him a strong man.

The general opinion of the appointment was well expressed in the *Freeman's Journal*: "It is no offence to Lord Frederick Cavendish to say that never was so small a politician appointed to so great a post at a crisis so important. . . . It is plain that Earl Spencer at the Castle will be the real head of the Irish Government, and that he will govern as well as rule."

Happy were the auguries of Nature for the new men and the new departure on May 6. The country and the capital were bathed in the glories of the early summer sun, when, shortly after seven o'clock in the morning, Earl Spencer arrived at Kingstown by the mail steamer, accompanied by his brother, the Hon. Robert Spencer, M.P., Lord Frederick Cavendish, and Mr. Courtney Boyle, his private secretary. The city was *en fête*. Those decorations in the form of flags, bunting, and triumphal arches, by which a people can manifest a joyous and enthusiastic welcome, were to be seen in profusion everywhere. But more gratifying still to the hearts of the new rulers must have been the

Caed Mille Failte of the cheering crowds which lined the route of the procession. At noon the Viceregal party were met at Westland Row Station by the Lord Mayor (Mr. Charles Dawson), and drove in state to the Castle. About the time the procession reached the Castle another event happened which gave further earnest of the conciliatory attitude of England—Michael Davitt was released from Portland Prison.

When the ceremony of swearing-in was over, the new Chief Secretary was engaged to a late hour in the afternoon with Mr. Thomas Henry Burke, the Under-Secretary, in connection with his various official duties. Some time after six o'clock Lord Frederick Cavendish left the Castle for his official residence in the Phœnix Park, and at about seven o'clock was strolling up the main road of the Park. Shortly afterwards Mr. Burke, who had been detained a little later in the Castle, came to the Park gate, and, as was his usual custom, got on the outside car of a man named Nicholas Brabazon, and this carman, without any instructions, proceeded to drive Mr. Burke in the direction of his residence, which is situated somewhat farther on than that of the Chief Secretary.

A little beyond the road leading to the Viceregal Lodge Mr. Burke overtook and recognized Lord Frederick Cavendish. Stopping his car, he joined the Chief Secretary, and the two proceeded to walk together up the main road of the Park. Far indeed were their thoughts from the imminence of a tragedy which was destined to shock the whole civilized world. As they passed just opposite the Viceregal Lodge, and had almost reached the turning in the direction of Chapelizod, they were set upon by a band of men, and in a few moments the Chief Secretary of a few hours' creation, and the tried and veteran Under-Secretary, were left upon the main road brutally done to death. The weapons used by the assassins were knives which, from the description of the wounds inflicted upon the two unfortunate gentlemen, were clearly of peculiar fitness for their murderous task.

Mr. Burke was stabbed through the heart from the back, the knife penetrating through the chest. There were two other wounds caused by a succession of stabs in the same region, and, in addition, his throat was slashed in two places and his left hand was cut. The injuries to Lord Frederick Cavendish were equally horrible. The bone of his left arm was completely cut in two, and the wound which, according to the medical testimony of Doctor Myles (now Sir Thomas Myles), was the cause of death, was a stab through the upper part of the right shoulder, which passed through the front of the shoulder - blade below the collar-bone, and severed the subclavian artery.

Their hideous work completed, some of the murderers sprang on to a car, and the remainder got into a cab, which were waiting in the vicinity.

The car was driven at a furious pace in the direction of the Chapelizod Gate, and the cab was quickly driven down the main road towards Dublin.

Many of Dublin's citizens were strolling about the magnificent recreation ground on that lovely summer afternoon, enjoying the Park's many attractions. A cricket match was being played upon one side of the road, and polo was in progress on the other side. But of all in the broad area of park, not one was sufficiently observant or alert to prevent what will be regarded for all time as a national calamity. Several persons saw the dreadful occurrence from a distance, and thought it was merely a scuffle, and it was not until they came up to the prostrate bodies that they discovered the true nature of the scene that had been enacted before their eyes. Meanwhile, the cab and car had disappeared. When assistance arrived, it was found that in the case of each of the unfortunate gentlemen life was extinct. The remains were at once removed to Steevens's Hospital.

CHAPTER XIX

AFTER THE MURDERS — THE INQUEST — THE MOURNING OF A NATION — THE NEW COERCION BILL

AT the Coroner's inquest the next day the evidence, in addition to that of Dr. Myles, was meagre in the extreme. A lad named Samuel Jacob was the first to reach the bodies. He had been bird-nesting in the fence surrounding the Viceregal Lodge, and had seen what he thought was horse-play or a wrestling match on the main road. The next persons to arrive were two gentlemen, named respectively Maguire and Foley, who were riding on tricycles, and Mr. Maguire proceeded to give the alarm. A moment or two later Lieutenant F. W. Greatorex, of the Royal Dragoons, came up. He had been exercising his dogs in the Park, and came out upon the main road at the Phœnix Monument at about a quarter past seven. Looking down the road, he saw what appeared to be a drunken quarrel going on, on the grass between the road and the footpath, and observed one of the group follow another into the middle of the road, and strike him, and knock

136

him down. He also saw a second man fall, and then the others jumped upon a car which passed Mr. Greatorex, and drove off rapidly along the road leading to the Hibernian Military School and Chapelizod.

This was all that could be told of the murder of two of the chief servants of the Crown in Ireland, and at the conclusion of the inquest, at which the Crown was represented by the Attorney-General, the jurors found the only verdict it was possible to find—namely, that Lord Frederick Cavendish and Mr. Thomas Henry Burke were "on Saturday, the 6th day of May, 1882, feloniously and of malice aforethought, killed and murdered by some person or persons unknown to us, the jurors." They added a rider, couched in the following impressive words :

"The jury cannot separate after this painful inquiry without expressing their extreme abhorrence of the awful and brutal murders which have disgraced our country, and while expressing their deep and heartfelt sympathy with the bereaved relations of the late Lord Frederick Cavendish and Mr. Thomas H. Burke, they desire to express a hope that the Almighty Disposer of events will enable the constituted authorities to discover the assassin or assassins, so that they may be brought to speedy justice. And we fully approve of the initiation of a subscription list, with a view of offering a substantial reward for such information as may discover and bring to justice the murderers, and we pledge ourselves to assist in this direction to the utmost of our power."

These solemn and prophetic words of the hastily summoned Coroner's jury well reflected the horror of the citizens of all creeds and classes at the dastardly deed done in their midst. I say " prophetic," for their prayer was granted ; but Divine Providence took its own time, and a few days after eight months had passed, nearly every member of the vilest conspiracy that had ever disgraced our country, including all those actually present at the murder, had been arrested.

When, on the Monday morning following the tragedy, the dreadful particulars became universally known, a thrill of horror and dismay pulsated throughout the civilized world. Two cries went up to the Almighty Disposer of events from the Irish people : the wail of a grief-stricken nation, and a prayer that the renewed friendship between England and Ireland might not be severed by the assassin's knife, and that the anarchic crime might not be laid at the door of the Irish people.

Throughout Great Britain there was a stern demand for vengeance. The people of the sister island were united in the opinion that it would take only a little time to reveal the connivance at, if not the actual participation in, the crime of the Irish leaders. Well might Justin McCarthy thus conclude his account of the dreadful episode in Irish history : "The Heavens should have been hung in black that smiling May day." And well might the organ of Irish national aspirations come forth to its readers upon that Monday morning, and tell them and the world how great a blow the advance to Irish liberty had sustained.

In an issue of the *Freeman's Journal* shortly afterwards came the manifesto addressed : "To the People of Ireland," signed by Parnell, Dillon, and Davitt. It stated :

" On the eve of what seemed a bright future for our country, the evil destiny which has apparently pursued us for centuries has struck another blow at our people which cannot be exaggerated in its disastrous consequences. In this hour of sorrowful gloom, we venture to give an expression of our profoundest sympathy with the people of Ireland in the calamity which has befallen our cause through a horrible deed, and with those who had determined at the last hour that a policy of conciliation should supplant terrorism and national distrust. We earnestly hope that the attitude and action of the whole Irish people will assure the world that assassination such as that which has startled us almost to the abandonment of our hopes for our country's cause is deeply and religiously abhorrent to their every feeling and instinct. We appeal to you to show, by every manner of expression possible, that amidst the universal feeling of horror which the assassination has excited, no people are so intense in their detestation of its atrocity, or entertain so deep a sympathy for those whose hearts must be seared by it, as the nation upon whose prospects and reviving hopes it may entail more ruinous effects than have yet fallen to the lot of unhappy Ireland during the present generation. We feel that no act has ever been perpetrated in our country during the struggle for social and political rights for the past fifty years that has so stained the name of hospitable Ireland as this cowardly and unprovoked assassination of a friendly stranger, and that until the murderers of Lord Frederick Cavendish and Mr. Burke are brought to justice that stain will sully our country's name." This manifesto was immediately disseminated throughout the entire country and posted up in the city.

In Parliament, upon May 8, Earl Granville moved the adjournment of the House of Lords, and speaking upon a similar motion in the Commons, Mr. Gladstone gave notice of the immediate introduction of measures for the repression of crime in Ireland. Even Parnell, sturdy fighter and creator of many an historical scene upon Coercion Bills, could only say : "I don't deny that it may be impossible for the Government to resist and to feel themselves compelled to take some step or other in the direction indicated by the Prime Minister."

On May 9 a great meeting of the citizens was

held in the Mansion House, and the speakers included the Lord Mayor (Mr. Charles Dawson) in the chair, Mr. Thomas Pim, Mr. James Talbot Power, D.L., the Rev. Provost of Trinity College, the Very Rev. Monsignor Canon Kennedy, P.P., Mr. Metge, M.P., Mr. J. F. Lombard, J.P., and Mr. Alfred Webb; and by the mouths of these distinguished men official expression was given to the horror and detestation of Dublin. On the same day meetings for a similar purpose were held by the Home Rule League and the Dublin Chamber of Commerce. It might be said with truth that there was not a public board or a gathering of men for any purpose throughout the country that did not pass similar resolutions in the strongest terms.

On the same day (May 9) Sir W. Harcourt introduced the new Coercion Bill, but in conciliatory and moderate terms, of which the following extract from his speech will give an idea : " All the body of Ireland is sound, but there is a frightful plague spot upon it, and I firmly believe that the Irish no less than the English nation desires that that plague spot should be removed. There is a cancerous sore in Ireland, and the House will anticipate that the great malady which corrodes and cripples its healthy frame comes from the baneful demon of secret societies and unlawful combinations. That being so, it is necessary that the surgeon's hand should cauterize and extirpate the disease, and to that operation I have to ask the attention of the

House to-night. . . . Every juryman—we need hardly wonder, and we can hardly blame him— looks with dread upon the levelled pistol at his heart, the dagger at his back, and the bullet of the rifle in his home at night."

The chief points of this most remarkable Bill might be summarized as follows :

(*a*) Its duration was to be for three years.

(*b*) Certain specified crimes were to be tried by three Judges without a jury. In such cases there was to be an appeal to the Court of Crown Cases Reserved, and an official shorthand note-taker was to be appointed.

(*c*) Extensive powers were given to the Executive to search for arms, and in certain circumstances to seize and suppress newspapers.

(*d*) Powers were also given to the Executive to arrest strangers, and it was made an offence to be out after dark without being able to give a good account of oneself.

(*e*) Finally, there were the powers given under the famous 16th Section, which I reproduce *in extenso* :

PREVENTION OF CRIME (IRELAND) ACT, 1882,
45 AND 46 VIC., CAP. 25.

16. Where a sworn information has been made that an offence has been committed, any resident magistrate in the county or place in which the offence was committed, although no person may be charged before him with the

commission of such offence, may summon to appear before him at a police-office or the place where the petty sessions for the district in which the said offence has been committed are usually held, any person within his jurisdiction whom he has reason to believe to be capable of giving material evidence concerning such offence, and he may examine on oath and take the deposition of such person concerning any such offence, and, if he see cause, may bind such person by recognizance to appear and give evidence at the next petty sessions, or, when called upon, within three months from the date of such recognizance; and the law relating to a witness, when summoned before a justice having jurisdiction, and required to give evidence concerning the matter of an information or complaint, shall apply to a witness summoned under this section.

(1) An offence for the purpose of this section means any felony or misdemeanour, and also any offence against this Act, with the exception of the offence specified in sections ten and eleven of this Act.

(2) A person summoned to appear under this section shall not be excused from answering any question on the ground that the answer thereto may criminate, or tend to criminate, himself, but any statement made by a person in answer to any question put to him on any examination under this section, shall not, except in case of an indictment or other criminal proceeding for perjury, be admissible in evidence against him in any proceeding, civil or criminal.

(3) A magistrate who conducts the examination under this section of a person concerning any offence, shall not, if such offence is punishable on summary conviction, take part in the hearing and determination of a charge for that offence, and shall not, if such offence is an indictable offence, take part in the committing for trial of such person for such offence.

On the day the Bill of 1882 was introduced, Mr. Trevelyan was appointed Chief Secretary. And in justice to the memory of Mr. Forster it should be stated that at this period of grave anxiety, and notwithstanding the fact that in the eyes of the public, both in Great Britain and Ireland, he was a discredited administrator, he came forward and placed his services at Mr. Gladstone's disposal.

His offer was not accepted, but nevertheless that fearless statesman did not hesitate to state—but with great moderation, considering the high position from which he had been driven by the relentless hostility of the Irish members—his opinion of the degree of their culpability. For on May 9, the day the Bill was introduced, in the course of his speech, and pointing towards the Irish benchers, he said : " Do not let the hon. members opposite suppose I think they instigated these assassinations. I do think, if they had set their faces as they now set them against past murders, we should not have had these murders."

The majority in favour of leave being given to bring in the Bill was 205, and in due course it became the law of the land. This Act, as I have stated, had by one of its sections a life of only three years.

In the year 1887, as a great part of Ireland still continued in a disturbed state, the Government of the day, with Mr. Arthur J. Balfour as Chief Secretary, introduced and passed a New Crimes Act, entitled the Criminal Law and Procedure (Ireland) Act, 1887, 50 and 51 Vic., cap. 20.

This Act, brought in by a Conservative Government, was in its essential parts but a poor imitation of Mr. Gladstone's Act of the year 1882, and I am quite certain that under its provisions I should never have been able to discover and bring to justice the perpetrators of the Phœnix Park murders.

Mr. Balfour was appointed Chief Secretary for Ireland in March, 1887, and the above Act became law on July 19 in the same year.

Under the provisions of this Act the Lord-Lieutenant, with the advice and assistance of the Privy Council, may from time to time proclaim any district of Ireland or revoke any such proclamation. All offences enumerated in the Act are only triable in Dublin district, by a Dublin divisional magistrate, and elsewhere by a court constituted of two resident magistrates, one of whom shall be a person of the sufficiency of whose legal knowledge the Lord-Lieutenant shall be satisfied. A power of appeal is given in all cases to the Recorders or Chairmen of Quarter Sessions sitting alone. Under its provisions and those of the Act of 1882, which contained similar sections, I had to try many such cases.

CHAPTER XX

PROGRESS AND FAILURE OF THE POLICE INQUIRIES—OUTRAGES IN THE WEST

MEANWHILE the police, under the direction of Mr. Mallon, Chief Superintendent of the Dublin Metropolitan Police Force, were making the most exhaustive investigations. It was not long before they had succeeded in tracing the car from the moment it left the scene of the outrage until, by a circuitous route, it reached Cork Street, where all traces of it were lost. Mr. Mallon reported that he much doubted whether, as was universally assumed in England, and suspected by many in Ireland, the outrage was the work of the Fenians.

Never, perhaps, in their history was such activity displayed by the police. As day followed day the newspapers chronicled arrests all over the United Kingdom, and for weeks dozens were daily detained and required to account for their movements. It almost seemed that by the process of exhaustion the perpetrators would be apprehended. At last, however, the public got so accustomed to sensational arrests, that the arrest of the morning was

146

expected to be followed, as a matter of course, by release in the evening. Some of the persons arrested under the Crimes Act as suspects, it was afterwards learned, were amongst the actual band of murderers, including James Carey, but these had to be released in the absence of evidence. Notwithstanding the offer by proclamation of a reward of £10,000, and a free pardon for information which might lead to the conviction of the murderers, it seemed that no one could be made amenable.

All sorts of stories were going the round, and rumours and clues of the most extraordinary and contradictory nature were everywhere eagerly discussed. Each morning brought some new story, often more fantastic than its predecessors, seldom not less ridiculous than the suggestions offered to the Government. There was a Southport story, in which a cattle-drover named Nangle informed the police that a canal boatman had told him that he could get £100 or £150 for a certain project. Upon investigation the boatman denied the story, and it was found that Nangle not only had contradicted himself, but was of too bad a character to be believed.

On May 19 the *Freeman's Journal* published a full confession of the murders by one who had taken part in them, and occupied the whole of their principal page in doing so. It was followed by a letter, purporting to come from the author, stating it to be a hoax.

Sir George Campbell, writing to *The Times*, suggested that the system used in India to put down Thuggeeism ought to be adopted for Ireland. The principal feature of this system seemed to be the offer of a free pardon to any person convicted of a Thuggee offence in consideration of the disclosure of information implicating others. A proposal such as this throws a lurid light upon the ideas prevailing in England about the character and propensities of the Irish people.

On May 18 the Crimes Bill passed its second reading by a majority of 383 to 45, and so widespread was the opposition to it amongst all classes that even the Judges, presided over by the Lord Chief Justice, passed the following resolution :

> "That the Prevention of Crimes (Ireland) Bill would seriously impair public confidence in the judicial office, and thereby permanently injure the administration of justice in Ireland."

It is not a matter for surprise, then, that Parnell and his followers showed the same dogged opposition to this Bill as they did to its predecessors. After many scenes and a multitude of amendments, twenty-five Irish members were suspended for persistent obstruction, and refused admittance to the House.

Shortly afterwards this Bill reached the Statute Book, and at a Commission of Oyer and Terminer for the City and County of Dublin, held early in August, Mr. Justice Harrison informed the Grand Jury that Mr. Baron Fitzgerald, who was to have opened the commission, had resigned because in his opinion the duties cast upon the Judges by the Act were unconstitutional.

Despite the Act and all the stringent, and, in the opinion of many, oppressive powers with which it armed the Executive, murder and outrage stalked through the land at noonday, and were as a pestilence that flieth by night. In the month of June two particularly atrocious murders were committed in the county of Galway. Mr. Walter M. Bourke, J.P., a barrister who had made a considerable fortune at the practice of his profession in India, and who had settled down as a landed gentleman, and his guard Corporal Wallace, of the Royal Dragoons, were shot dead on the highroad at Ardrahan. Mr. Bourke was a Catholic, and had earned some considerable notoriety by attending Mass at Carraroe Church with a repeating rifle, and would not leave the church even at the request of the clergyman.

Towards the end of the month Mr. John Henry Blake, agent to the Marquis of Clanricarde, who was being driven in company with his wife by a servant-man called Ruane, was shot dead, as also was Ruane, about half a mile from Loughrea, by an ambuscade lying behind a stone wall. The day before, Patrick Cahill, caretaker on the Ballyseedy estate, was murdered in Seville Place, Dublin, for, it was thought, disclosing information in connection with some secret society.

In August several remarkable events took place. In the beginning of the month an agitation began in the Royal Irish Constabulary, for better hours and pay. On the 15th the O'Connell statue was unveiled. On the 16th Mr. E. D. Gray, M.P., High Sheriff of the City of Dublin and editor of the *Freeman's Journal*, was sent to prison for three months and fined £500, and bound over in bail of £10,000 for his good conduct, by Mr. Justice Lawson, at the City Commission, for certain articles reflecting upon the juries at the Commission. The freedom of the city of Dublin was conferred upon Parnell and Dillon the same day.

Two days later a dreadful massacre—for nothing else it can be called—took place at Maamstrasna, near Cong. Some six months before two bailiffs had disappeared from Lord Ardilaun's estate, and it was rumoured about the locality that a family named Joyce knew what had become of them, and could give evidence implicating certain men in their murder. On the night of August 18 John Joyce, his wife, his married son and his daughter-in-law, and two children, were murdered in his cottage under the most revolting circumstances. In this case, however, justice was satisfied, and on the eve of the Christmas following three men suffered the extreme penalty of the law in Galway Jail.

The reader must be somewhat surfeited with this dish of stale politics, but it is a necessary, if rather heavy, *hors d'œuvre* to the greatest event of an eventful life—an event of national importance. Those set in judicial authority, of no matter what degree, save the brethren of the unpaid bench, are debarred from politics, and I had settled down to the quiet life of a Dublin police magistrate, and to the compulsorily impartial contemplation of the events taking place about me. As an Irishman I was grieved by the dreadful state of affairs prevailing throughout the country, and naturally, if only from my acquaintance with the men of the moment, I took a great but necessarily concealed interest in the tempestuous politics of the time. Little did I think, however, that the key of the Park mystery was to be entrusted to my hands, and that on me would devolve the task of uncloaking one of the vilest conspiracies of history : bloody in its objects ; indifferent to the laws of God or man in its attainments ; hideous in the almost unimaginable repulsiveness of the character of its leading members. No more dreadful task could fall to the lot of any man, for, when the terrible tale was told, justice demanded the lives of five, the lifelong imprisonment of four, and less but severe punishment for seven.

By the end of the month of August the public excitement in reference to the tragedy had died down. Almost four months had passed, and the assassins were still at large, and it seemed that the murders were to be relegated to the long category of undis-covered crimes. On August 30 Mr. Mallon reported the result of his inquiries to the Castle authorities, and, when several months after I came to consider his report, I was satisfied that at that time he was not able to bring guilt home to any of the parties who rested under suspicion. He had seen and examined a great number of witnesses, includ-ing Godden, a Park ranger, the two cyclists Fry and Meagle, and a man named Ladley, who were all in the Park on the evening of May 6. Godden gave a full description of the men on the car, but Mr. Mallon's comment was that it was " suspi-ciously accurate." He reported that none of them gave more than mere general information as to the car and horse. Yet as it happened, and as it will appear farther on, all these men were able to give most important evidence.

Mr. Mallon thought so little of the evidence of Meagle that he suggested that he and Fry must have been under the influence of drink, or that they made up the story, and suggested that it was a plant to confuse. Yet Meagle was able afterwards to identify the most ferocious of the group of men whom he passed, and it was his evidence which afforded me the clue which led to the unravelling of the whole plot. Mr. Mallon also said he thought nothing of Ladley's evidence, though when that witness was produced later on

by Mr. Horne, his evidence enabled me to discover
the witness Glynn, who proved the guilt of James
Carey, as hereafter set out.   The cabs in the Park
on May 6, Mr. Mallon reported, had been all
accounted for.   Yet the cab which brought and
took back one of the assassins and two of his co-
conspirators escaped notice.

During the week following the murders, Mr.
Mallon was informed, after the manner in which the
police often receive valuable information (which,
though it generally leads to the detection of an
offender, is not provable in a court of justice in our
country), that five men, named James Carey, Daniel
Curley, Patrick Brady, Edward McCaffrey, and
Kelly, whose Christian name was not given, were
amongst the assassins.   Later he heard that two
other men not since named were of the gang.   Later
on he heard that James Carey, Daniel Curley, the
cabman, and a fourth man not since named, were
the principals ; that Carey and Curley were always
mingling with workmen, and their movements could
not be traced on May 6.

In a further report, dated October 28, in reply
to a statement of the authorities in London, that
a man called Kavanagh, who had recently been
arrested and discharged, was the man who drove
the car, Mr. Mallon said : "I have to report that
there were two carmen named as having each
driven two gentlemen to the Polo Ground on
May 6.   First Nicholas Gorman, and second

Michael Kavanagh. The first-named drove two
commercial travellers to the Park, then to the
North Star Hotel, Amiens Street, and he left the
Park soon after six o'clock. *Neither* of these two
carmen would answer the description, and they
have no car or horse like the one described. I
think suspicion rests upon Michael Kavanagh,
because he has been in America."

It is only fair to Mr. Mallon to state that his
failure to apprehend or adduce evidence against the
murderers was not due to any lack of detective
ability. Against such a powerful organization as
was afterwards discovered to exist, held together
not only by oath but by fear of death, it was impossible, with his limited powers, for Mr. Mallon to
take effective measures. However much he might
suspect a party, he had no power to arrest him, nor
to put to him any question. Thus, many of the
Invincibles who were arrested with others as suspects
under the Coercion Act, 1881, had, as I have said,
to be discharged, there being no evidence against
them. Of Mr. Mallon's ability I shall speak again
later.

It is now time for me to tell how I came to discover the clue which led to my being appointed to
investigate the murders by, and the assassination
conspiracy of, the Invincibles.

CHAPTER XXI

THE OUTRAGE UPON MR. FIELD—MY APPOINT-
MENT TO INVESTIGATE IT—THE CLUE—
"AH! YOU VILLAIN!"—APPOINTED TO
INVESTIGATE THE PHŒNIX PARK MUR-
DERS

On the evening of November 27, Dublin was again
horrified by the report that a most brutal attack
had been made in Hardwicke Street on Mr. Denis
J. Field, a well-known and respected citizen.
Mr. Field was returning to his private residence in
North Frederick Street, and when he came to the
corner of Hardwicke Street, just at his residence he
was attacked by a body of men, and received several
stabs and other injuries, two of the stabs passing
through his mouth and cutting his tongue, and it
was only by feigning death that he escaped with
his life. His assailants then jumped up on a car
that was waiting, and disappeared. The only
reason which could be assigned for the attack was
the fact that Mr. Field had acted as a juror in a
case involving the capital charge which was tried at

the Winter Assizes in Green Street in September, and in which the prisoner was convicted.

Some few days after the attack, as one of the Divisional Justices of Dublin, I received an order from His Excellency the Lord-Lieutenant to hold an inquiry under Section 16 of the Prevention of Crimes (Ireland) Act, 1882, into the circumstances attending the attack upon Mr. Field. Under that section, which I have already quoted in full, a magistrate, when so directed, had power to inquire into crime, and summon before him and examine upon oath all parties whom he might deem expedient, even though no person had been actually charged with the crime. I may say that it was realized by this time in Dublin that a criminal conspiracy of very serious magnitude, and with the most malignant objects, existed in the city.

I sat for the purpose of the inquiry in a small chamber in the Lower Yard of Dublin Castle. The room was in full view of a public-house belonging to a man called Wren, and, as it afterwards transpired, Wren's was the principal meeting-place of the Invincibles—the name which the conspirators gave their body.

On my first entry into the room, I found there a man from the Board of Works nailing down a carpet for my use. On his departure, Mr. Boulger, whom I had brought with me from the police courts, and whom I found to be a most efficient officer, asked me if I had remarked the wicked scowl which the man laying the carpet had given me. I replied that I had not. I found afterwards that he was one of the Invincibles, and was the man who pointed out Mr. Burke to his murderers.

After the lapse of some days, during which several witnesses had been examined by me, Mr. Field came before me and detailed the particulars of the terrible mutilation to which he had been subjected. In the course of his evidence he informed me that the man who stabbed him in the back had called out in so doing, "Ah! you villain!"

I at once remembered I had seen these words not long before in connection with some criminal matter or other. The question was, Where and what was the matter? I proceeded to search my memory, and on referring to Mr. Mallon's report of August 30, I read in it that a cyclist named Meagle, in passing by the scene of the murder, told Mr. Mallon that he heard one of the men attacked, in what he considered a scuffle only, call out, "Ah! you villain!" I thought that probably Meagle was mistaken in attributing the words used to the party attacked, and not to the party attacking. Having regard to that expression used on both occasions, and to the similarity of the mode of attack, I at once came to the conclusion that the men engaged in the attack on Mr. Field were the same as those engaged in the murders in the Phœnix Park. At the most it was a clue, but to me it was a certain conclusion that it was one and the same gang that was responsible.

As my warrant only empowered me to inquire into the attack upon Mr. Field, I reported my views to Lord Spencer, and asked him to extend it, so as to include the murders in the Phœnix Park. His Excellency said he would only be too pleased, as they had long since given up any hope of discovering the perpetrators or bringing home guilt to them. At the same time he assigned to assist me Mr. A. E. Horne, R.M., representing the Constabulary, and Mr. Mallon, representing the Dublin Metropolitan Police Forces. Mr. Horne had been making inquiries, but nothing did or could result, because, like Mr. Mallon, he had no power to swear witnesses. When I have brought the reader through the various clues I had to pursue, it will be apparent, without my asserting it, that much of the success which attended my investigation was due to the ability and efficiency of these two gentlemen. I had also a shorthand note-writer, an excellent young officer, Mr. William Irvine, who, I am glad to hear, has since risen to a high position in the Force.

CHAPTER XXII

THE SECRET INVESTIGATION—MY PERSONAL
RISK—ROBERT FARRELL'S CONFESSION—
THE ARRESTS

UPON receipt of my warrant I immediately set
myself to examine the police records since May 6,
to which I have previously referred. None of these,
however, suggested to my mind that the police had
any real suspicion which might lead to proof of the
identity of those implicated in the murders. I then
proceeded to call before me every person whom
Mr. Horne or Mr. Mallon had ascertained to have
been in the Park that day. Every clue, no matter
how trivial, was eagerly followed up, and as a
necessary consequence, time and time again I found
myself balked and compelled to retrace my steps.

From the first the police authorities hinted that
it was the work of the Fenian organization, and
I spent many days working upon that clue, but in
the end I found that, though the organization was
very widespread, it was in no way responsible for
the murders. Many of the leading Fenians who
came before me expressed what I knew to be

genuine horror at the crime, and as a matter of fact I derived very material assistance from them in the course of my inquiry.

Gradually I formed a suspicion as to the parties responsible, if not actually implicated ; and at the same time I came to the conclusion that they were recruited from the Fenian body. My conclusion proved to be absolutely correct; I came afterwards to know that the Invincibles, as they styled themselves, were of necessity all Fenians who had formed themselves into an Inner Circle. They became, so to speak, an excrescence upon the original body, and were at the time of which I write altogether outside its rules and objects.

I had before me nearly all the Invincibles. They, of course, denied everything. Nevertheless, I was able to extract a little of the truth from each of them. When it came to the point of calling before me those whom I suspected of being the actual murderers and those in command of the body, my position was indeed one of extreme danger. I was well aware that these men looked upon my action as one intended to break up their conspiracy and to bring home guilt to the guilty. In plain words, I was engaged in fixing the rope about their necks. It was abundantly clear that, if I continued to endeavour by cross-examination to extract the truth from a band of desperate men who were already in a most perilous plight, and knowing that they must have been aware that I knew more about them than I pretended to know, my life would be hourly in jeopardy. Accordingly, I suggested to Mr. Samuel Lee Anderson, the Chief Crown Solicitor for Ireland, that under the circumstances at this stage the Crown should be represented before me. To this course the Crown assented, and instructed as counsel one who has since risen to the highest eminence in his profession—Mr. Stephen Ronan, now Lord Justice of Appeal. That learned gentleman, upon consideration, came to the conclusion that the Crown had no right to be represented before me, and so upon myself alone was cast the discharge of the dangerous and disagreeable duty of examining the various witnesses. Indeed, during the whole of the investigation no questions were addressed to any person who was brought before me, save and except by myself.

Captain Talbot promised me ample police protection, and from that day out the guard which I had from the beginning of the inquiry was more than doubled. Next morning my wife was startled to find upon leaving the house a number of police patrolling the grounds of my residence; this they continued to do by day and night for many months. For nearly eight years I was under constant police protection wherever I went.

One of the Invincibles who was examined before me, and who denied everything, but at the same time had unwittingly been giving me a good deal of information, told me that I should be very cautious going home from the tram to my residence. I then lived at Riversdale, Terenure, a house which is situated at a distance of three or four hundred yards from the end of the tram-line. I told him I was quite safe, as I had a constable always with me. Next morning a man who, though an Invincible, had taken no part in the murders in the Phœnix Park, nor in the attack on Mr. Field, and who had also given me information as to their movements, came to me and said : " Mr. Curran, you are very foolish. You told the man who was before you yesterday that you had only one constable with you when going home from the tram to your house. After leaving you, he called a meeting of the men, and told them they would be able to put an end to the investigation by attacking you on your way home from the tram, as you had only one constable to protect you."

I eased his mind by informing him that I had three men with me from Dublin, and that on my way home at night, when passing the Rathmines Barrack, midway between Dublin and Terenure, on a signal from one of the three a telegram was sent to the Barrack at Terenure, and upon my arrival there, instead of having only one man with me I had quite a number.

I knew the man to whom I had falsely given the number of my guard to be a Fenian, and only surmised that he was an Invincible ; and I purposely told him I had only one constable with me, as I felt certain, if an Invincible, he would communicate that fact to his fellow-conspirators. This man afterwards pleaded guilty before Mr. Justice O'Brien to the charge of conspiracy to murder Mr. Field, and was sentenced to ten years' penal servitude.

Little by little I examined, compared, and pieced together, the evidence and the facts admitted by the men summoned before me, and I was soon in a position to make up a list more or less correct of the names of the conspirators and the objects of their conspiracy. As I have said, I had nearly every member of the gang from time to time before me, and the danger of my position was not a little increased by the fact that I had no power to order them to be searched when entering the room. Having regard to the opinion of Mr. Ronan, I personally examined, and cross-examined when necessary, every witness who came before me, whether Invincible or not, and delegated my authority to no one. For my own safety when engaged in examining, I took the precaution of keeping my right hand in the side-pocket of my coat, and in it I held a revolver at full cock with my finger on the trigger.

I next called before me a man against whom I had evidence proving that at all events he was a leading Fenian ; his name was Robert Farrell. In the course of my examination, in the presence of

Mr. Mallon, I put certain questions assuming all my suspected facts to have been proved. Farrell appeared to be very much surprised, and a few days later, on January 3, 1883, he went to Inspector Kavanagh and told him, from his interview with myself and Mr. Mallon, he was sure that someone had turned traitor and had given us information which had led to my questions. He further said that he did not intend to be left in when others were turning informers, and then made a statement which he signed, giving full details of the conspiracy and the names of those engaged from time to time in carrying out its objects. Mr. Mallon brought the statement to me, but said that the man was afraid to come before me a second time in the Castle, as all the members of the gang were well watched going in. It was then arranged that Mr. Mallon should bring the man to my residence late at night on January 11. Mr. Mallon and Farrell came to my house as arranged that night, and before they left, Farrell had sworn a deposition before me. It was dated January 12, for it was after midnight when it was sworn.

By this time I had become aware that a terrible organization existed in Dublin, its object being to murder all tyrants—in other words, all Government officials. I had more than a suspicion of the names of those engaged in the attack on Mr. Field, and in the Phœnix Park murders. I had all of them brought before me a second and third time. Each of them was beginning to look on his neighbour as turning traitor. They were becoming desperate, one suspecting the other.

Upon consideration of the contents of Farrell's deposition and of the various facts within my knowledge, and after he and Mr. Mallon had left on the early morning of the 12th, I came to the conclusion that, as matters stood, no Government official, no Judge, nor indeed anyone in authority, was safe from assassination while these men were at large, and that the lives of Mr. Horne, Mr. Mallon, and myself were in special danger. I left home that morning determined, in the interests of public safety, to arrest every member of the body that night.

On my arrival at the Castle, I called on Mr. (now Sir George) Jenkinson, Assistant Under-Secretary for *crime*, to inform him of my intention, but he was out. I then went to the Attorney-General, now Sir Andrew M. Porter, Bart. (he was afterwards Master of the Rolls), and explained to him my object. He asked me to give him all the depositions made before me, and to call back in a couple of hours. I did so, but before I saw the Attorney-General I saw Mr. Mallon, and ascertained that he, as well as Mr. Horne, thoroughly agreed with my views. Mr. Mallon informed me that a very hot interchange of words had just taken place between the Attorney-General and Mr. Jenkinson. I then met the two gentlemen. The Attorney-General was very irate that he had not been informed of the

evidence that had been given before me. Mr.
Jenkinson, on the other hand, contended that it was
very unfair to force his hand, as he could produce a
witness who could prove the entire case. I asked
why the witness had not been sent before me. I
may add that I examined this witness on a subsequent occasion, but did not believe a word he
swore. He was afterwards charged with arson,
committed in various parts of the county Dublin.
As the Attorney-General and Mr. Jenkinson were
in direct disagreement as to the necessity for the
immediate issue of the warrants, the Attorney
agreeing with my views, they arranged to refer the
matter to Lord Spencer.

Accordingly, I adjourned until late at night, to
enable them to consult His Excellency at the Viceregal Lodge. This they did, and returned with his
answer. Lord Spencer's orders were, that if I
thought I had a good case, I was to act on my own
discretion. I did act upon my own discretion, and
late that night, with the approval of Mr. Horne
and Mr. Mallon and the consent of the Attorney-
General, I signed warrants for the arrest of every
man whom I knew to be an Invincible in Dublin.
These were some twenty-seven in number, and
included a member of the body who was sitting in
the room helping me, but whom, at his own suggestion, and for his own safety, I found it my duty
to arrest also.

By breakfast-time next day the majority of them

were safely under lock and key in Kilmainham Jail.   This wholesale arrest was very advantageous in another direction.   My experience of the criminal law has been considerable, and that experience tells me that in cases like the one with which I had to deal, and when the evidence is nearly altogether that of approvers, it is almost impossible to obtain corroborative proof until the parties charged are in custody.   Fear of personal violence makes witnesses in cases of conspiracy unwilling to come forward until the conspirators are in custody.   For instance, in Mr. Field's case, a young woman who knew Joseph Brady, one of the principal members of the gang, witnessed the attack.   Brady came to her afterwards, and warned her that if she said she had seen him, she would meet with the same fate as Mr. Field.   It was only when she saw him in custody and felt safe from his threats, that she fully identified him.

In concluding this chapter, it is only right to say in connection with the arrests that, although my opinion prevailed over that of Sir George Jenkinson, he subsequently continued to act with me in the most loyal manner.

CHAPTER XXIII

THE UNRAVELLING OF THE INVINCIBLE CONSPIRACY

NOTWITHSTANDING the confession of Robert Farrell, I was still a long way from being able to establish the identity of the members of the Invincible Society who were responsible for the murders of Lord Frederick Cavendish and Mr. Burke. Nevertheless, Farrell's information was of great value. It enabled me to lay hands with some certainty upon its members, and then I was enabled by piecing up fragments of evidence and by conjecture to set about obtaining evidence against those whom I knew to have been in the Park, and suspected as having participated in the murders.

In a much condensed form Farrell's story was this : About the year 1876 he was sworn in as a member of the Fenian organization by a man called Joseph Flood. Later in the same year the man called Curley became the head centre of his circle, and in the month of June of that year, Curley told him in his house in Mount Street that there should be an inner or confidential circle formed, to consist of "the cream of the Society."

The oath administered to Farrell upon joining the Fenians was as follows : "I, Robert Farrell, do hereby swear that I will serve the Irish Republic now established, that I will take up arms at a moment's notice, and will implicitly obey all lawful orders of my superiors, and I take this oath in the true spirit of a soldier."

It will be apparent later on that a much more stringent form of oath was administered to the members of the Inner Circle. The first duties assigned to Farrell, after he became aware that the Inner Circle existed in reality for the murder of Government officials, were minor parts in the series of remarkable attempts upon the life of Mr. Forster. It was afterwards deposed that they were nineteen in number, and all happily were unsuccessful.

On one occasion they arranged to attack Mr. Forster as he was driving in his carriage along the Quays from his lodge in the Park to the Castle. Carey was stationed at the Park gate with orders to wave a white handkerchief when Mr. Forster passed through the gate. A second man was to repeat the operation when the carriage passed him. Farther on lay a band of the Invincibles waiting to do their dread work. The second man failed to give the signal, and the carriage with Mr. Forster in it drove safely through their midst.

On another occasion Mr. Forster was in the Castle. Outside in front of the *Express* newspaper office was a cab and white horse, in charge of the man who afterwards, in the same cab with the same white horse, drove some of the murderers out to the Park and back on May 6. An Invincible was stationed at the Castle gate to give notice to the cabman of the approach of Mr. Forster's carriage. The cabman had instructions to drive in front of the carriage if Mr. Forster was in it. The body of the Invincibles was waiting to attack anyone in a carriage preceded by a cab and white horse. The notice from the Castle gate was duly given, and the cab drove on in front of the carriage containing Mr. Forster. Again the Invincibles were to fail; for, when turning round from Parliament Street to the Quays, the white horse slipped and stumbled to his knees, and before he could recover the carriage passed on in front. The cabman did his best to overtake it, but was unsuccessful, and the carriage once more passed through the Invincibles, and Mr. Forster escaped.

Their final opportunity came when it was announced that Mr. Forster was to leave Westland Row Railway Station for Kingstown, on his way to England. When the hour of the departure of the train came, the entrance to the station was crowded with the men, some armed with pistols and others with knives. The carriage arrived as expected, but to their disappointment only two

ladies alighted.   It afterwards appeared that earlier
in the day Mr. Forster met a friend who persuaded
him to drive to Kingstown and dine there with
him, and meet Mrs. Forster at the boat.   And so
Mr. Forster escaped being murdered in the presence
of his wife and daughter.

Farrell also told me of an attack that was
planned against Mr. W. G. Barrett, of Kingstown,
a gentleman who had acted on the same jury as
Mr. Field.   A letter was to be handed to Mr.
Barrett in Westland Row by one member of the
gang, and whilst his attention was so engaged,
others were to attack him with knives.   Fortunately
this attempt miscarried, in consequence of the
absence from home of Mr. Barrett.   From Farrell
I also learned that the man Delany who had been
arrested in connection with the attack upon Mr.
Justice Lawson was also an Invincible.

In the face of such information I think the
reader will at once see the good sense of my
decision to arrest the whole body.   Once under
lock and key the difficulty of obtaining evidence
was appreciably lessened, and soon I was able to
form a pretty shrewd idea as to who were the
actual participators in, or at least the parties present at, the Park murders.   At last I arrived at
the conclusion that these men were James Carey,
Joseph Brady, Timothy Kelly, Patrick Delany,
Thomas Caffrey, Michael Fagan, Daniel Curley,
Joseph Hanlon, and Joseph Smith ; and that a

cabman named James FitzHarris, and a carman named Michael Kavanagh, had driven the bulk of the assassins to the Park and back again upon the completion of their dreadful enterprise.

The ascertainment of the names was but a small matter compared with the great task I had now before me of collecting sufficient evidence to satisfy a jury of the guilt of these men. Practically the only evidence I had now was that of the informer Farrell, and of some others of the gang who were willing to turn approvers. The law in its wisdom suggests that no man ought to be convicted upon the uncorroborated testimony of a confederate in the crime who has turned approver. Though this statement is hardly correct as a rule of law in such cases, it is correct as to the practice of Judges, who warn juries not to convict on the uncorroborated testimony of informers alone. I had at least by independent witnesses to place the men in the Park on the afternoon of May 6, and then let the informers tell what happened.

I am not going to take the reader through the evidence adduced against each prisoner. That in itself would need a volume very nearly the size of the official report of the trials, which I have now in my possession, and which runs into nearly a thousand pages. (There are, I may add, only about five copies in existence.) I merely purpose giving a short account of the three principal members—Curley, Fagan, and Carey, sketching how I traced out the evidence necessary to support the informers' statements as to the complicity of these men in the murders. In the cases of other members of the organization it was not difficult, once we had them under lock and key, to find plenty of corroborative proof. I shall tell how Carey came to turn King's evidence, and his story of the murders, at which he was not only present, but was indeed one of its principal instigators.

Daniel Curley was the chairman of the Executive of Four of the Irish Invincibles, of whose constitution I shall speak in more detail hereafter. He had been arrested as a suspect during the early part of the year 1882, but was discharged. He was a very soft-spoken gentleman, and once, when answering some questions I put to him in the course of my examination, asked me how I could suspect him of such an atrocious crime, as he was a married man with a wife and children. I merely replied, " That remains to be seen."

After seeing his devilish work in part accomplished, he walked back with one of the men to the cab, in which he returned to Dublin. In doing so he met his doom ; for facing him on his way was a young woman whose positive evidence of identification was the sole corroboration of the informer, and consigned Curley to the gallows.

The following are the means by which we traced that young woman :

Shortly after I had commenced my investigations

Mr. Horne came to me one day and told me he had heard a rumour that a woman, coming to see a servant in the Viceregal household, had been a witness to what she thought was a scuffle in the Park, and in consequence was so much frightened that she turned back. I caused inquiries to be made in the Viceregal household among the servants, but none of them remembered any such occurrence, and for a time the matter dropped.

Some time afterwards Mr. Horne came to me, and, reminding me of what he had told me before, said that he had again heard the rumour, but this time it was among the servants in the Chief Secretary's Lodge. He further said that a constable under him had heard it from a Park ranger. I sent for the ranger, and questioned him about the matter. At first he denied all knowledge of it, but at length he admitted he had heard it from his daughter, who was a servant in the Chief Secretary's Lodge. I at once sent a cab to the lodge, with a request for the attendance of the housekeeper. She came in to me looking very frightened, and wondering what she was wanted for. She told me she recollected that one of the servants was expecting a friend to come to see her on May 6, and it was said that the friend had turned back on seeing a scuffle in the Park. The girl's name, she told me, was Charlotte Noakes. She had left the service of the Chief Secretary, and had returned to England, and the housekeeper did not know her whereabouts, and had no means of ascertaining her present address.

In reply to me she stated that they had parted good friends. "If that is so," I said, "she must have written to you announcing her safe return." "That may be," the housekeeper replied, "but I have no distinct recollection."

I requested her to return to her residence, and make a search for such a letter. In a couple of hours she came back brandishing in her hand a letter in which it appeared that Noakes had gone back to her father, who lived in Devizes, in Wiltshire. I immediately wired to the Chief Constable in Devizes to ascertain if there was such a man, and if his daughter was living with him, and, if that were the case, to find out from her the name and address of the girl who had been coming to see her on May 6. I further asked the Chief Constable, if he found Charlotte Noakes, to send her over to Mr. Mallon. Next morning we had a wire from the Chief Constable saying he had found Charlotte Noakes, was sending her over, and that the name of the girl was Emma Jones, who was then in the service of a lady in Carlisle. I then sent a sergeant of the Royal Irish Constabulary, under Mr. Horne, for Emma Jones, and told him not to come back without her. At the same time I wrote to her mistress that there was no charge of any kind against the girl, and that she was required only as a witness.

A few mornings later Emma Jones appeared before me. She told me she saw the scuffle, which very much frightened her, and that while it was going on two men walked back from it towards her. The face of one man was indelibly imprinted upon her memory. She could not be mistaken. The man was Daniel Curley. The jury believed her, and Curley was hanged. Miss Jones identified one other member of the group, and also the man who drove the cab.

At first I had little or no corroboration of the informer's story in the case of Michael Fagan. One morning Mr. Horne brought me a message from Dr. Carte, the prison doctor, saying that one of the Invincibles had informed him that when they were lying on the grass, waiting for the arrival of Mr. Burke, a soldier and two civilians walked by, and one of the civilians nodded to Fagan.

I was aware, from my inquiries, that a number of sappers had been in the Park that day, and accordingly I wrote to the General in command of the regiment, requesting him to ascertain whether one of his men had been walking that day with two civilians shortly before the murder, and if they had passed a group of men on the grass, to one of whom one of the civilians nodded. Next morning a soldier came to me with a letter from the General. The General stated that he had paraded the regiment, and had explained to them what I required, and that the bearer of the letter, Private Sandford, immediately stepped out of the ranks and said he recollected the matter. The General placed the private at my disposal, and the latter gave me the names of his two friends. On inquiry from Mr. Mallon, I ascertained that they were Fenians, and were well known to the police. They lived at the north side of the city, and at that time were working as compositors in the office of a Dublin newspaper.

I knew it would be useless, and only put them on their guard, if I summoned them or searched for them at their address. I found out from the manager of the newspaper that they would come in to work at eleven o'clock that night. I returned to the Castle at that hour, and sent down a couple of constables, who asked for one of them. On his appearance the constable told him that I wanted to see him, and asked him to come to the Castle, and this he agreed to do. A similar course was adopted in the case of the second man, who also consented to come.

I examined them apart, and for a long time they refused to give any information or to admit that they were in the Park at all on May 6. I then confronted them with Private Sandford, and then with each other. At length they admitted the truth of the private's statement that he had seen them nod to one of the group, and further admitted that the man was Fagan. Before they left the Castle that night they had sworn and signed a

12

statement to this effect. Their evidence subsequently led to the conviction of Fagan.

When the Invincibles were placed in the dock, Private Sandford identified another of them as a member of the group he had passed in the Park. That member at once offered his services as a Crown witness, and was accepted.

CHAPTER XXIV

JAMES CAREY TURNS INFORMER

JAMES CAREY was a member of the Dublin Corporation, and posed as a respectable member of society and a man given to piety. He was most assiduous in the discharge of his religious duties as a Catholic, and was a member of a confraternity attached to a church in Dublin. At the investigation before the magistrate in Kilmainham he spoke strongly about the indignity of being charged with such a crime. He even went so far as to instruct a solicitor to write me a letter threatening me with an action for slander. The only evidence against him was that of the informer, and he continued to protest his innocence until the appearance of a certain witness in court. We obtained the services of that witness in the following curious manner :

Among the great number of witnesses examined by me was a gentleman named Ladley, who was produced first by Mr. Mallon and subsequently by Mr. Horne. This gentleman told me he thought he could be of no assistance to me, but related the following incident : While standing looking on at the

179

polo match in the Park on May 6, Mr. Ladley got into conversation with a stranger who was engaged in like manner. While they were so chatting Lord Spencer passed up, and the stranger said: " That's a good man. I remember one winter paying five shillings to skate on the pond in the Zoo, and leaving it disgusted, as the ice was rotten. I then took a walk in the Park, and met a gentleman, who asked me where I had been skating. He brought me into some private grounds containing a grand sheet of ice. The gentleman stood on the bank while I was skating, and I asked a man near who he was. The answer was, "Lord Spencer."

The evidence was so far unimportant, but the witness went on to say that after telling this story the man crossed to the main road of the Park, and spoke to one of two men who were sitting on a seat. This latter fact was very important, because I was aware that Carey and another man who belonged to the Board of Works occupied such a position just before the murders. I determined to find that skater.

For some time there appeared in the Dublin papers a short advertisement asking the gentleman who, after leaving the Zoo, had been allowed by Lord Spencer to skate in his private grounds the preceding winter, to communicate with the Under-Secretary in the Castle. Some time afterwards, and whilst the magisterial investigation in Kilmainham was proceeding, on my arrival in the Castle one morning, I was handed by Mr. Mallon a letter from a party writing from Carlow, saying that he recollected the circumstance stated in the advertisement. I wired him to come up to the Castle. I saw him next morning, when he informed me that the man to whom he had spoken when leaving the polo ground was James Carey. The name of this informant was Glynn.

By a strange coincidence the entrance of this witness into court was immediately followed by Carey's offer to turn informer. I strongly opposed his being taken as a witness, as I considered we had ample evidence without having to rely on his testimony. He was one of the leaders and paymaster of the gang, and I was quite sure that, according as they were identified in the dock, less prominent members of the Invincible Society would offer themselves as approvers. This afterwards proved to be the case. It was a matter of *sauve qui peut* with most of them. Counsel for the Crown took a different view—I do not say wrongly. They were of opinion that the fact of a man of Carey's position turning King's evidence would be a warning to all who might in future engage in similar conspiracies.

Carey left the dock for the box, and there told a story than which there can be no more revolting in the history of crime. The earlier part of it, which concerns the formation and the constitution of the Invincible Society, I have considerably compressed. The latter part, in which he described the preparations for the murders, and the murders themselves, of which he was an eyewitness, I reproduce in his own callous words.

In 1861, or 1862, Carey became a member of the Fenian organization, and remained so until the year 1881. Up to that time the body seems always to have been in debt, and the only business it transacted was the preparation for a war upon England, and the trial of traitors to the body. In November of 1881 a man called Walsh, from the North of England, came to see Carey to obtain his assistance in the formation of a "society that would make history." Carey acquiesced, and Walsh proceeded to administer an oath to Carey, which was sworn upon a knife, which Carey held in his right hand and Walsh in his left. Part of the oath was in the following words: "That I, of my own free will and without any mental reservation whatsoever, will obey all orders transmitted to me by the Irish Invincibles, nor to seek nor to ask more than what is necessary in carrying out such orders, violation of which shall be death."

Walsh then informed Carey that the number of the Society in the United Kingdom would be about 250 members, of which the Dublin quota was not to exceed fifty. A governing body of Four was constituted for Dublin; one of the body was elected chairman, and the remaining members were Carey, Edward McCaffrey, and Daniel Curley.

The chairman was afterwards arrested as a "suspect," and Curley becoming chairman, Joseph Brady was co-opted a new member of the Council. Walsh gave them a list of persons who had been put on the list in London to be "removed." Mr. Forster's was the first name, and Lord Spencer's the next, and Mr. Burke's was added afterwards. Walsh left them a bag of fifty sovereigns, with directions to enrol a sufficient number of men from the Fenian body.

This they did, and in their method of recruiting lay my greatest difficulty in unravelling the conspiracy. I ascertained that each member of the Council of Four swore in new members, but the new members only knew the man who swore them in, and another, their Right and their Left. As a consequence they only became gradually aware of the persons of their brother conspirators ; and then only by meeting them from time to time when directed by one of the Council to attend at certain places for the purpose of "removing" some obnoxious person.

A man called Captain McCafferty took over control after Walsh, and he in turn was succeeded by a mysterious individual, known as "No. 1." This man was agent to the parties in England who supplied the knives and the money. Of the latter he appeared to have an unlimited supply, for a day or two before the murders he promised to let the Society have £1,000 if it wanted it.   In reality

"No. 1" had been a small shopkeeper in Kingstown. We never managed to lay him by the heels, for, upon hearing of the arrests, he escaped to London, and managed to elude the vigilance of the London police, who had my warrant for his arrest.

When Mr. Forster finally escaped all the attempts upon his life, "No. 1" ordered the gang to confine their attentions to Mr. Burke.

The following is Carey's evidence dealing with the murders :

"On the evening of the 5th of May, that we were to meet at King's Bridge, I was at the Royal Oak Tavern in Parkgate Street. From the window of that place I saw some of our men assemble. They were about twenty in number. They were about the bridge in groups scattered about. Brady and Curley were there that evening. Martin was not there, he was in gaol. Tim Kelly, Thomas Caffrey, Paddy Delaney, Joseph Mullett, two Hanlons, were all there. I think that's all I recollect. I don't remember Fitzharris being there. I don't think he was. James Mullett was not there, he was in Dundalk Gaol at the time.

"The man William O'Brien I have mentioned is the O'Brien in the dock. I never heard his name till I heard it here. One of the two Dwyers was also there—one of them had gone to America.

"They continued to wait about the place about an hour that afternoon. Mr. Burke did not appear that evening. An arrangement was made about being there at ten o'clock next morning.

"I drove towards the place next morning. Fitzharris drove me in the cab. On my way up, on the quay opposite the chapel on Arran Quay, I saw a Mr. Burke walking with two gentlemen. It was on Usher's Quay, and I was on the same quay. The three gentlemen passed me, going in towards town.

"I got out of the cab after I saw them. I told Fitzharris to go on to King's Bridge, and tell the men there that he had passed. I was not perfectly acquainted with Mr. Burke's appearance then. It was his brother, I think, that I saw. It was the wrong man; none of us knew Mr. Burke's appearance, I think, except Joe Smith, a man who used to work about the castle for the Board of Works.

"After three o'clock on that Saturday, the 6th May, I saw Joe Smith. I met him, and he coming out of the Castle. I spoke to him. He was going to be paid his week's wages. I did not wait for him. I told him to meet me afterwards. He came across a little after three to Wrenn's public-house. I watched for him.   There were others there of our members.

"There were there the occupants of the car and Daniel Curley. That is, those who were afterwards the occupants of the car—Joseph Brady, Timothy Kelly, Thomas Caffrey, and Patrick Delaney.

"The horse and car were at this time in Dame Street. It was there all day. Kavanagh was there with it, of course. The horse and cab were there portion of the day. I left the cab at half-past ten, and two of my children in the cab. He went on to King's Bridge, and I told him to tell Curley Mr. Burke was passed. Then he had to go home with my children.

"I next saw the cab near Sycamore Alley, about one o'clock, and Fitzharris with it. I think he had a brown horse—it was not a white one, anyway.

"When I met Smith after he was paid, he went to get his dinner with Daniel Curley and the other men who were present, at Flemming's. Smith did not get his dinner till the other men came back.

"Curley went with him, and paid for Smith's dinner. The Smith I speak of is Joseph Smith. I saw Kavanagh that day getting drink in Wrenn's. Very little drink was going on, though. I saw Kavanagh there. After that I recollect getting into the cab. I recollect it well. It was down at the corner of Essex Street, facing the bridge. No one was in it when I got in it.

"Joe Hanlon, this Smith, and myself got in it. Fitz-harris drove us from that place. I had seen the other men going towards the car, which was standing at Sycamore Alley when I left.

"In the cab we drove on straight along the quays on the left-hand side, [and crossed King's Bridge. It was ten minutes to five o'clock when we left Parliament Street in the cab. Having crossed the bridge, the cab went in straight through the Park gate.

"On our way from Parliament Street to the Park gate, I did not see the car with the others. After we entered the Park, the cab first pulled up opposite the near end of the polo ground, a little above the Gough Statue.

"We three got out of the cab there, and after a few moments I went over to look at the polo match, and the other two stopped there where the cab stopped.

"After that I believe two of our party drove up on a car. Curley was there. I did not see how he came there.

"I afterwards saw Michael Fagan in the Park.

"I stopped at the polo ground until Curley came to me. Curley said: 'What are you doing here?' I replied: 'I am looking at this game. I never saw it before.' He said: 'It's not here you should be; you should be over; you can't tell the moment he might be coming up.'

"I then went with him to where Smith was. He was sitting on the seat convenient to the road, on the right-hand side as you go up.

"I sat there with Smith. Curley told me he would send the car down. He went up in the cab. I did not see him getting in the cab.

"Curley said it would be better for to have the car there below for me to give the signal. Smith was to stay with me to point out Mr. Burke, but Smith did not know what he was wanted for at the time. I'll save every innocent man I can.

"I know Mr. Glynn the builder. I know him well. I served my time under him, and saw him examined here. I was speaking to him on that day for a quarter of an hour nearly. I recollect seeing the car coming down that Curley said he would send back to me. Kavanagh was driving it. He pulled up right opposite to me, to the seat where I was sitting. I did not speak to him. He turned the horse to the roadway, and proceeded to feed the horse, putting a nosebag on him.

"Kavanagh was right enough at that time—at the time I got on his car—but he got excited afterwards. He appeared to me afterwards to be excited when we stopped afterwards. I did not see that he was frightened; it is from what I heard. After he put the car in the way I have described, I did not notice any car come up.

"After Mr. Glynn went away, Smith drew my attention to someone. Glynn went away at a few minutes past seven.

"At ten minutes past seven Smith said to me, 'Here's someone coming,' and he got up and went four or five yards in a diagonal line towards the road. 'Here's someone; here he is,' he said, and he made from that towards the road. I saw no car at all.

"Smith said, 'Come on,' and he made for the car, I being twelve or fifteen feet behind. Smith told Kavanagh—of course, I did not know his name—to be quick. 'Hurry up! hurry up!' and Kavanagh took off the nosebag, and Smith and I got on the car.

"Before we got on the car I looked over the top of the car—putting my foot on it—and saw two gentlemen together. I and Smith got on the same side of the car, and went on straight up towards the Phœnix. I was on the front seat, next the horse, on the pathway side, the left-hand side as you go up.

"On the way up on the car I had a handkerchief in my hand—a white one. That was the prearranged signal.

"On the way up, and before we stopped, I recollect

passing two persons sitting on a seat. One of them was a constabulary man, and the other was a civilian—apparently a recruit. They were about two hundred yards from where we stopped.

"We passed Fitzharris's cab before we stopped. It was on the right-hand side when we passed it.

"When we stopped there were seven men where we stopped. They were scattered into about three groups. I can give the names of seven.

"They are Joseph Brady, Timothy Kelly, Patrick Delaney, Thomas Caffrey, Michael Fagan, Daniel Curley, and Joseph Hanlon.

"When we came up they were all on the footway. Of course, they knew I was coming: they had seen the handkerchief.

"Dan Curley had control of the arrangements there. Kavanagh stopped.

"Brady and Curley came over to me where I was on the car, and I leapt off. Curley asked : 'Well, is he coming ?' and I said : 'Yes, the man in the grey suit.'

I leapt off, and Smith stopped on the car. He did not know what to do. He did not know what the business was. I asked Joe Brady, 'What about this man ?' and he said : 'Tell him to go off to hell out of that.' I went over and told him to go home, and he did so.

"He went off in the direction of between Island Bridge and the Hibernian Schools, and after that Kavanagh drew up a bit above the place we were, and then he was bid to come back.

"After that there was a consultation between Brady, Curley, and I.

"I asked Brady what was I to do. 'You may go,' said he; 'you are not wanted here.'

"Before I went I said : 'Mind, be sure, the man in the grey suit.'

"I started then on a diagonal line for Island Bridge, and before starting the two gentlemen were two hundred yards away, coming up.

"Kavanagh, with his car, were on the road right opposite. He had been higher up, but he was made to draw back.

"I looked back and saw the two gentlemen come up with the men I had left there, when I was about two hundred and fifty yards away.

"At the time the gentlemen were approaching the men I did not see a car pass down from the Phœnix. I heard it from Joe Brady afterwards.

"When the two gentlemen came up to where this collection were, they were allowed to pass them.

"When I was about two hundred and fifty yards away from the place I had left those men, I had looked round occasionally before that, and at that distance I looked, and I seen the seven meeting the two.

"The first three were abreast—Curley, Fagan, and Hanlon; about twelve feet after them Kelly and Brady, and about six feet Delany and Caffrey.

"I seen them meeting—the two meeting the seven. The two passed through the ranks. They let them pass through.

"When I seen that, I went on a few steps further, when I looked round, and seen a right-about movement made by the last four.

"I went on a few steps further, and I looked again, and I seen the two men in the rear getting to the front and closing on the two first men—the two gentlemen. What I seen then I'll describe it.

"I seen one figure coming in collision with the two gentlemen. The one in the grey was on the inside.

"I then saw this man, Joseph Brady, raising his left hand, and with his left hand striking the gentleman in the grey suit. That's all I seen.

"I then made for Island Bridge. It was seventeen minutes past seven o'clock when I left the pathway. About twenty minutes past seven it was all over. I looked at my watch; I timed my own movements accurately that day.

"After I came out by the Island Bridge gate I went into Coady's public-house at Kilmainham. I met Smith before that. He ran after me when I was inside the Park gate, and I gave him a couple of matches. I did not bring him into Coady's.

"We came home on a tram. I had told Smith to meet me at the tram. We went to College Green on the top of the tram. I brought Smith into Cleary's public-house in Grafton Street. I made myself seen by Mr. Cleary. I had known him before. I shook hands with him and talked to him for half an hour. I timed myself there. It was ten minutes past eight. Brady afterwards told me that there was a car passing down at the time they met the gentlemen first. He said there was a gentleman on the car passing by at the time.

"Curley was at my house that night. He called about half-past eight o'clock. I was not there; I came in about nine. I met Curley at the corner of Holles Street. Before that I was across at Mrs. Stafford's. When I saw Curley I said to him: 'Is it true what I hear, that Lord Frederick Cavendish and Mr. Burke are killed?' 'It is,' said he, 'so I believe. I cannot tell whether they are killed or not, of course.'

"Curley then described what he had seen. He said: 'When I seen the two men pass through the four, I and the two men turned round, and thought there was going to be another failure.'

"Those three were armed with revolvers. I could not tell who had knives. I know who had two knives. That was Joseph Brady. I could not tell from whom he got them; he had them the day before.

"Curley said in continuation: 'I seen that they closed up on the two gentlemen, and I seen Joe Brady attacking one gentleman, and following the other on to the road, and attacking him also. I seen him coming back from him to the other party, and then I seen him wiping the knife in the grass, to take the blood off it, off the knife. I stood still until I seen them all on the car.'

"He said that when Joe Brady came back to the other body, the body was lying on the ground.

"He said that Joe Hanlon, Fagan, and himself went away in the cab. He said they drove down straight to the Gough Statue, and that one of the velocipede men followed them down, but that he was covered by two revolvers, and that the cab turned off towards Phibsborough at Gough Statue towards the Constabulary Barracks, and that they got out there, and that he, Curley, went straight to the *Express* office and put a card into the letter-box, stating how it was done, and the next day he went with the same to the *Irish Times, Freeman*, and the *Irishman*.

"I saw the cards. On the card was written, 'Executed by order of the Irish Invincibles.'

"I met Brady about ten o'clock or after the same night. 'Is it true,' said I, 'about Lord Frederick Cavendish being that strange gentleman?' and he said, 'I don't know who it is.'

"He then told me how it happened. I asked him why did he let Mr. Burke pass at first, and he said there was a car passing, and that when they turned right about he followed Mr. Burke and put his hand on his shoulder, and then stabbed him. 'With that the strange gentleman struck me with his umbrella, and called me a ruffian. With that I got annoyed and excited, and I struck him in the arm, and then followed him out into the road and settled him there. When I looked round, I saw Tim Kelly at Mr. Burke.' Mr. Burke was on the ground when Brady had left.

"Brady continued, saying, 'Tim Kelly was coming away from Mr. Burke. He left him, and I went to him and cut his throat.'

"'Were you so cool,' said I, 'that you wiped the knife in the grass, as Curley was telling me?' 'I did,' said he, 'and threw them up on the car, and got off.'

"I remember after that Curley, Brady, and I meeting with the man No. 1, at M'Caffrey's house. No knives

were there then. We got the history in full from Joe
Brady. He went over it for the stranger, No. 1.

"We adjourned then, and the knives were produced at
the next meeting, about a week or ten days afterwards.
Joseph Brady produced them. This man, No. 1, gave
directions to have them destroyed. It was not mentioned
how. I thought bad of destroying them. I wanted to
send them to the Exhibition. The knives were broken up
into little bits, and the handles burnt to ashes, and the
dust produced to No. 1. Some one of the Invincibles
told me that. I was in as a suspect at the time."

CHAPTER XXV

CONSPIRACY AND PIETY

JAMES CAREY will in all probability go down to posterity as the prince of informers. All conspiracies are fraught with the ever-present danger of a member turning informer. Usually such a man is one who has joined in weakness, and from a similar cause informs upon his fellows. Carey was not such. He was a leader, and organizer, and the paymaster. He enrolled the members, planned the crimes, took charge of the knives. It was he who, with a white handkerchief in his hand, called out to the men in the Park when the two unfortunate gentlemen were approaching them: "Remember the man in the grey suit"—indicating Mr. Burke as the man who was to be murdered, and in the end left his human instruments to pay the terrible penalty. I cannot speak with moderation of the character of James Carey. His life and his story speak for themselves. The corporator and man of public affairs plans anarchy and the destruction of society. The pious man who receives the most sacred mysteries of the Catholic Church contrives and contemplates one of the most abominable sins in the Christian code. It cannot be said that he was immoral. He was non-moral. He had not even that shallow sense of honour that is said to obtain amongst criminals. He was a man with an object. It might be good or bad, but, for its achievement, men of Carey's type could see no difference between right and wrong. Murder was his object, and by a diabolical conspiracy he achieved it. Safety from the consequences which the law attaches to it was his next object, and that, too, he secured.

He was a very self-sufficient man, and had no conception of the baseness of his acts, whether as conspirator, murderer, or approver. On his cross-examination by the late Judge Webb, who defended Joseph Brady, he took up the attitude that his action was one eminently deserving of credit from both sides. At one stage, when Judge Webb was pressing him, he said: "I am more friendly to you, Mr. Webb, than you think; bear that in mind." Another time, in reply to a taunt from one of the prisoners, he said: "I am doing my best for you." His best!—the saving of his own life at the expense of his accomplices!

Long before the trials I was personally aware of the character of James Carey, as the following incident will show: The contract for constructing sewers in Dublin had, much to the dissatisfaction of the city workmen, been given to a Scotchman

named Stansfield. Carey had considerable influence
with the workmen, and, at his direction, some of
them covered up in certain places some bad work.
Carey complained that the contractor was putting
in bad work. An inquiry was demanded and
granted, and the Inspector was brought by Carey,
as if by accident, to the various places where the
bad work had been done. Mr. Boyd (now Mr.
Justice Boyd) and I appeared for the contractor
and sub-contractor, and at the end of the inquiry
Carey's villainous plot was proved beyond doubt.

Carey, as might be expected, had no regard
whatever for the sanctity of an oath. After the
trials had concluded a man was arrested, whom
I knew to have brought over the knives to Ireland.
Carey, of course, knew him, and informed me that
he could positively identify him. I happened to be
absent next day when the case was called in the
police court. On my return I was informed that
the man had to be discharged, as Carey swore he
did not know him at all. I saw and questioned
Carey as to what he meant by his conduct. His
reply was: "Of course, Mr. Curran, I knew and
recognized him, and swore I did not. But you
must remember that I shall not always be here,
but expect to go out once more a free man, so I
had to do something to soften the people outside,
who feel resentment against me, and who are sore
at my having given evidence."

One day, when the trials were over, he asked to

see me in Kilmainham, and suggested that, as he had gone through a great strain, he considered he was entitled to some relaxation, and that he would like a short trip. I pretended to agree, and told him I should send Mr. Mallon with him, and that he should select where he would like to go. He replied that Killarney would be a nice trip. Mr. Mallon came to me afterwards, very indignant at the proposition, and was very considerably eased in his mind when I told him I had no such intention, and that I was only laughing at Carey when I made the suggestion. It was not the imminent danger of such a trip that influenced Mr. Mallon; it was pure disgust at the proposed companionship.

I never had any occasion to doubt Mr. Mallon's courage; there were many plots against his life. On one occasion he went at my suggestion in company with another to a foreign port, disguised, and at considerable risk to himself, to identify an individual, of whose identity it was important that we should be satisfied.

I have also always borne testimony to the important part played by Mr. Mallon in the unravelment of the tangled Invincible plot. His splendid detective capacity and his skill in the command of a big police organization were well known to me. It is only right that in these reminiscences I should express my hearty appreciation of the work done by him. At the same time I must be allowed to add an expression of regret that he has allowed to creep into his book, "Irish Conspiracies"—recollections of John Mallon (the great Irish detective), as produced by a Mr. Frederick Moir Bussy—many statements in regard to my work which are both misleading and inaccurate.

Joseph Mullett was a mad enthusiast, with most perverted notions of right and wrong. While taking a leading part in the Invincible organization and plotting the murder of various parties, either officials or jurors, he was at the same time most assiduous in attending to and practising his religious duties as a Catholic, and most constant in invoking the assistance of the Almighty and of many saints to help him and strengthen his arm in working for his country. He was one of the very few of the body who imagined (however misguidedly) that justice was on their side, and demanded their action. Of the objects and aims of the great majority in the organization, the less said the better.

After Mullet's arrest the police found in his house a number of documents, which were proved to be in his handwriting. These included the following letter, which appears to be a copy of one written by him, the copy being in his handwriting, and which speaks for itself:

"DEAR J.,

"One of the Emmets is still in Dublin, and, as I told you before, he is one of the greatest traitors ever stood in shoe-leather. He stops somewhere in South King Street, and I hope you may be able to make an example for the rest of *cuare* fellows of the band. You know Jack Love well; that's the man, and I hope you will not forget this at once, as I am asked to write to you about it.

" Don't forget my letter of yesterday.

" Yours truly,

" J. M.

" He has the Emmet suit on him. Will you take it off and send it home; it cost a lot of money."

The police also found in his house a diary kept by him, which showed how greatly upset were his ideas of right and wrong.

In tracing the movements of the men whom I suspected to have driven away on the car on May 6, I had before me an old lady, to whose house Brady had gone after the murder, and immediately after his arrival in Dublin. She swore positively that Brady was in her house on that evening at an hour which, if she was swearing the truth, would have rendered it impossible for him to have been at the scene of the murder. She was positive as to the exact time, and in reply to me, she said she knew it by the clock, which she looked at just as he entered the house.

I asked her was she quite sure.

" Yes, sir," was her reply.

" And you looked at the clock and saw the hour."

" Yes, sir."

"Now kindly tell me what o'clock it is by the clock over the fireplace," pointing to it.

She had to admit she could not tell, as she did not know the hours on the clock. She was very angry on leaving at having been caught, and her language was not quite nice.

After I had concluded the investigation into the Phœnix Park murders, I happened to be in London, and, as usual, paid a visit to my friend Sir Robert Anderson. I went with him to see Sir William Harcourt, and when with him, we were joined by the Attorney-General, Sir Henry James (now Lord James). I had to give both a full account of my doings during the investigation, and I found them most kind and agreeable.

While in London I strolled one day into the Court of Appeal, where Lord Fitzgerald was sitting. Immediately on seeing me, he sent his tipstaff to me with a note, asking me to fix a day on which I could dine with him. I did so, and had the honour of being introduced to Lady Fitzgerald. There were several bigwigs there, including a Scotch Law lord. Then once more I had to relate many of the incidents of the investigation.

The late Inspector Kavanagh, D.M.P., gave me most valuable assistance in the Phœnix Park investigation. I have referred to him already in the account given of it as the officer to whom Robert Farrell made his statement after the interview with

Mr. Mallon and myself. Kavanagh was in consequence an object of grave suspicion and hatred to the body of Invincibles, and had to be protected by members of his own force, and to go about armed.

On one occasion, when in company with his escort, a man ran past them, followed at some distance by a crowd shouting, "Stop, thief!" Kavanagh, forgetting his position, and mindful only of his instincts as a policeman, darted after him alone, but when just about to overtake the thief, he tripped and fell, a revolver in his pocket going off, and the bullet lodging in his arm. The man, turning round, and seeing what had happened, stopped his flight, resuming it only after he had put Kavanagh sitting up and made him comfortable. Thereby I lost the services of a valuable assistant. History is silent as to what became of the good Samaritan.

Both Mr. Justice O'Brien and Mr. Justice Murphy took a great interest in my success, and were very anxious to see me rewarded for the results achieved through the Phœnix Park investigation. Judge Murphy spoke to me frequently as to the probable legal vacancies, and Judge O'Brien did likewise.

Judge Murphy came to me one evening at the Castle, and told me Lord Spencer wished to see me, to thank me in person for my success in the investigation into the Park murders. I told my friend that, as Lord Spencer had already written thanking me and praising my courage and success, I did not require further thanks, as I had only done my duty. I then left and went home. Some few days afterwards, at a Castle concert, at which my wife and I were present, the Judge came to me again. He insisted upon my going up to His Excellency. This I had to do, whereupon the Viceroy again warmly eulogized my work.

It is a matter of keen pleasure to me to know that this Judge's son, Mr. Edward S. Murphy, who, I may say, commenced his professional career before me in the Midland Counties, has rapidly sprung into business, and gives every promise of a distinguished career.

CHAPTER XXVI

KERRY

WITH the verdicts of the citizens empanelled on the various juries sending the conspirators to their punishment, and the universal satisfaction that tardy justice had at length avenged the tragedy of May, 1882, my dreadful task in connection with that calamitous chapter of Irish history was completed.   Lord Spencer thanked me in the name of the Government, both in person and by letter, and, as a further mark of confidence, entrusted to my hands the distribution of nearly the whole of the reward of £10,000 offered for information leading to the apprehension of the conspirators.

Very shortly after I had concluded the investigation into the Phœnix Park murders I received a telegram from the Attorney-General, telling me the position of Chief Justice in Jamaica, worth £2,500 per annum, was vacant, and asking me if I would like to accept the post.   I consulted my wife, who was very nervous and anxious as to my personal safety.   I then wrote, saying I should be glad to accept the position.   I was all the more inclined to go out to Jamaica as an old friend and co-circuiteer was out there as puisne Judge. I refer to my namesake, Charley Curran. Just about the same time I received a letter from Lord Spencer, saying that in consequence of the death of Mr. Elrington, Recorder of Derry, there was a vacancy on the County Court Bench, and offering me the appointment, but adding that, if I refused it, he should know the reason (referring to the Jamaica offer). I consulted two friends at the Bar—the late Mr. Justice Murphy and the late Mr. Justice William O'Brien. Both of them strongly advised me against going out to Jamaica, the latter using some very strong language about what he called my folly in thinking of the foreign appointment. So I wrote to Lord Spencer, thanking him, and accepting the position of County Court Judge.

Judge Neligan, then Judge in the Midland Counties, went to Derry as Recorder, and in the autumn of 1883 I succeeded him in the Midland Counties, where, in later times, I spent so many pleasant and happy years.

In the month of October, 1886, the late Lord Ashbourne sent for me, and told me the Government was most anxious that I should consent to go to Kerry and try to restore peace in that county. It was well known that for some time prior to the end of the year 1886 Kerry had been in a very disturbed state. Murders were very frequent, and boycotting was prevalent. The late Judge O'Connor

Morris, who was Chairman of Quarter Sessions for the county, was a most amiable gentleman, a most accomplished writer, but very visionary, and much more of a theorist than a practical man, and was very pleased when offered the opportunity to turn his back on County Kerry. Even the solicitors practising before him began, so to say, " to lose their heads," judging by the frequent scenes in court appearing in the newspapers.

The County Court Judges in Ireland, unlike their brethren in England, have fixity of tenure, and cannot be moved except with their own consent. However, I consented. I first made the condition that after I had done my best in Kerry, I was to go back to the Midland Counties on the first vacancy.

That year I had to revise the Parliamentary roll twice. I had concluded my revision in the Midland Counties, and found that I had to commence that of Kerry.

When first I went to that county I had the benefit of the advice and assistance of Sir Redvers Buller and Colonel (now General) Turner. No such scenes as were reported to have taken place before Judge O'Connor Morris took place before me. On the contrary, I found the practitioners a most able and courteous set of gentlemen, and I never had a word of difference with any one of them.

Here, perhaps, I may tell a little story of the late Daniel MacGillicuddy, Crown Solicitor, who was a

very good fellow, and did his work very well. One
morning he came to me at my house at Terenure, in
a very depressed state, saying that the Attorney-
General, afterwards Lord O'Brien, had sent for him
the previous day, and dismissed him from the post
of Crown Solicitor. He begged of me to go and see
the Attorney-General, and intercede for him.

It appeared that a leading merchant of Tralee
had been charged before Cecil Roche, R.M., with
some trivial offence, but one which came within
the Crimes Act. There was a point of law which
the Attorney-General wished to have decided by
the Lord Chief Baron, who was expected to preside
at the approaching Assizes, and Mr. MacGillicuddy
had positive instructions to have the case sent on
for trial, and not allow it to be summarily dealt
with. Cecil Roche, however, refused to comply
with the direction, and adopted his usual course
of sentencing the party to one month's imprisonment—a course which gave the defendant no right
of appeal. The course was most extraordinary
considering the position of the party charged.

I went at once to the Castle, and saw the
Attorney-General. He seemed very angry over
the matter, and at first point-blank refused to
consider the decision, saying that as a result of
Mr. MacGillicuddy's action he had been obliged
to discharge the party convicted. I pointed out
that that was a very strong course to adopt, and
said I hoped he had a medical certificate. He

stared at me full in the face, and there was the slightest drooping of one of the eyelids, which told volumes. The discharge was, in fact, due to such a certificate. I pointed out that it was more Cecil Roche's fault than that of the Crown Solicitor. His reply was that MacGillicuddy should have protested more strongly than he did.

In the end I softened his heart, which was never very hard, and he agreed to reappoint Mr. Mac-Gillicuddy, but upon the sole condition that I should give an undertaking in writing that he should in future obey all orders, which I did. Perhaps that undertaking is still among the Castle Records. I need not say I sent my friend, who was waiting for me in the Castle Yard, home with his heart gladdened.

I went to Kerry with a very bad character. My advent was heralded there by the statement that I was "The Head Inquisitor of Dublin Castle." Every man passing me on the road, driving or walking, met me with a scowl and a look of defiance. Before I left Kerry, at the end of five years, I was able to say that I had satisfied the wants of both landlords and tenants to a very considerable extent, and I was presented with an illuminated address by the magistrates and others in Kerry, headed by the Roman Catholic Bishop, the most Rev. Dr. Coffey, entreating me not to leave Kerry, and praising my action. In place of the scowl which met me when I first went into the county, a pleasant smile and "God bless your Honour" greeted me wherever I went.

During the greater part of my time in Kerry it was in a very disturbed state, and the moonlighters were very active. Two of the ringleaders in one of the most disturbed districts were prosecuted under the Crimes Act and sentenced, each of them, by the magistrates to six months' hard labour. They appealed before me, and, the evidence being very convincing, I had to confirm the conviction. I was, however, satisfied that the sending them to prison would not result in the district being made more peaceable, so I informed them that I would not sentence them till the following Quarter Sessions, but that I should remit the sentence if, during the next three months, no criminal act was reported to the police as having taken place within a radius of ten miles from where they lived. I explained to them that they fully deserved the sentence, and so was not making them responsible for the acts of others, as I was satisfied they were ringleaders, and could keep their neighbours quiet, and I was giving the latter an opportunity of helping them out of their difficulty.

At the next Quarter Sessions the Head Constable reported to me that the district had been in a most peaceable state, and that the defendants were as good as any two policemen in keeping the district quiet, but that there would be no further danger if I again postponed judgment till the following sessions. This I did, with the result that that part of the county became so accustomed to be quiet and without crime that all parties forgot their old bad habits. I adopted a similar course in a case in Westmeath, with the same satisfactory result.

In the bad times, especially when members of the Land League got beyond control of its leaders, it was difficult to get jurors to convict, even upon the clearest evidence. When I first went to Kerry I found juries had been in the habit of deciding cases, not in accordance with the evidence, but from fear of the consequences and the dictates of self-protection. The contest was sharp and decisive, and before I left the county I had the satisfaction of knowing that all their verdicts were above suspicion. I always considered they were not so much to blame, living, as they did, in solitary parts of the counties, open without redress to terrorism and night attacks.

This, which was true of Kerry, was equally so of the Midland Counties, and the following case will show how correct my views were: In one of the Midland Counties a father and several sons lived together, and a local trader, being unable to obtain payment for provisions supplied to the father and partaken of by all, sent the Sheriff in, to seize under a writ of fi. fa. The Sheriff seized a number of sheep on the land. These were immediately claimed by the sons, who by force retook possession of them from the Sheriff, and the latter had to abandon the seizure. The sons were all sent for trial before me for rescue, and were defended by counsel. It transpired that the prisoners had recently joined the Land League.

The case for the Crown was proved very clearly. Having regard to the framing of the indictment, I refused to put to the jury the question of property, but left them three questions to answer :

First, Did the Sheriff seize the sheep by power of the writ of fi. fa.? To which they answered, "Yes."

I then asked them, Did the prisoners retake possession of the sheep from the Sheriff. To which they answered, "Yes."

I next asked them, Was the retaking of the sheep from the hands of the Sheriff by force and arms; otherwise, was it done with violence? To which they also answered, "Yes."

I then directed them in accordance with those findings to convict the prisoners. They retired, and after some time returned, and to the surprise of many, but not to mine, brought in a verdict of "Not guilty." I was quite satisfied, having regard to their answers, they were honestly intending to do their duty, but were deterred by fear of the consequence to themselves individually from bringing in a final verdict of "Guilty." I told them I should release them from all responsibility for the verdict, and struck out the word "not," and sentenced the prisoners to six months' imprisonment each. A

14

complaint was immediately made to the Castle and
to the House of Commons.

I refused, as I was entitled to, to take notice of
any such complaints. An application was then sent
to the Lord-Lieutenant by the father, for remission
of the sentence. With that I was of course obliged
to deal, and in so doing set forth all the above
facts. The Law Officers, I understood, were of
opinion that I was quite justified in my action,
and His Excellency refused to interfere with the
sentence.

CHAPTER XXVII

MAGISTRATES AND LICENCES

WHEN first appointed Chairman of Quarter Sessions I found, both in the Midland Counties and in Kerry, that publicans' licences were to be obtained, and were granted without much difficulty, in Kerry especially, some of its towns being chiefly composed of licensed premises. Canvassing went on to a very considerable extent, and local influence was brought to bear. In this county, as also in the Midland Counties, magistrates of the landlord class, provided they had a friend to serve, were just as anxious to grant a licence, I found, as the more humble magistrates.

In one case a man who had taken a house from a local landlord applied for a publican's licence. It was refused by the magistrates who ordinarily attended the sessions on the ground that it was not required, though they were willing to grant it to him simply as an hotel licence, which he re-fused.

The application was renewed at the next sessions,

when magistrates who had not been present at the
previous sessions, and many of whom had never
attended—some coming from distant parts of the
county—were present. These had been canvassed
openly, and some were driven in a carriage to
court by the applicant. One of the magistrates I
knew had been going round for days canvassing. It reminded me more of an election. I asked
one gentleman what brought him there. His
reply was that he came with others to vote for a
licence.

I took my seat on the Bench, and, looking round
the court, said: "I refuse to preside at such a
packed Bench," and retired to my chamber. I told
the clerk of the Crown and Peace to take no order
from any magistrate in my absence. A magistrate
proposed that one of them should take the chair,
but Mr. Huggard explained that no one could do
that except myself. Their indignation can well be
pictured. After they had all left, I announced
that if the man applied at next Quarter Sessions,
and not a single magistrate present that day
attended, I should consider whether I might not
grant him an hotel licence.

An application was subsequently made in the
Queen's Bench for a mandamus to compel me to sit
and hear the case. In reply I made an affidavit,
going seriatim through the list of those present,
specifically stating my reasons for objecting to their
presence on the Bench to hear and determine the

case solely on the evidence before them. I need not say nothing more was ever heard of the conditional order.

Next Quarter Sessions only one of the magistrates—one who had taken a strong part on the previous occasion—attended. He now insisted on his right to sit. I replied that of course he had the right, but if he did so, I should adhere to my former ruling, and, as a result, there could be no order. I was asked to retire for a few minutes. On my return I found the gentleman had departed, and the licence was granted.

In one of the Midland Counties a young lady, a member of a county family, thinking she might do business on her own account, obtained a spirit grocer's licence for the gate lodge and carried on business as a grocer in it.

After some time she considered she might better her position by obtaining for the house a full publican's licence. Nothing could have been more objectionable than the house and its position. It was opposed on every ground by the police. The applicant was examined by her solicitor, and in reply to some questions put by me, admitted that she wanted the licence to better herself. She also naïvely stated she had canvassed many of the magistrates who were on the Bench, and that some of them had promised to support her application and vote for her. She did not seem to think there was anything wrong in her action.

I requested the magistrates to come into my chamber and consider the matter. They did so, there was some straight talk, and, to the surprise of the applicant, the application was refused on the grounds of objection urged by the police.

When sitting at the Licensing Sessions in a town in Meath, a magistrate of the county came hurriedly on the Bench, and asked me to call on a particular case. In reply to me he informed me that he had been requested by the solicitor for the applicant to vote for his client, which he wished to do, but admitted that he did not know the applicant. I refused to take his vote under the circumstances, and told the solicitor, who was in court, that I should have him removed unless he made the magistrate leave the Bench, which he did, and so his assistance was lost to the applicant.

On another occasion, in the same county, Mr. Knight, the clerk of the Crown and Peace, informed me before going into court that a friend of an intended applicant had informed him in his office that he had made it all right with the magistrates, but that he was anxious that Mr. Knight should endeavour to propitiate me, and offered to give him five pounds if he would try to do so. Mr. Knight turned the man out of the office, saying in a joking manner that the sum of ten pounds was the least amount I should require. When I entered the court I found, as I expected, the Bench fully packed. After the case had been opened, and when the applicant was on the table giving evidence, I held out my hand to him, saying : "What about the ten pounds you promised to give me if I did not oppose your application." I then told the Bench of his disgraceful suggestion to Mr. Knight, and commented strongly on the impropriety of canvassing magistrates, and said I hoped that no one sitting with me had been approached as Mr. Knight had. The fear of such a suspicion attaching to them put an end to their anxiety to help the applicant. By adopting such means and course of action, after some years I quite killed the system of canvassing by intending publicans which I found so very prevalent in all four counties.

The unlimited supply of whisky at wakes is a constant cause of much of the crime in Ireland. On the death of any small farmer a friend or relation would go to the nearest publican and order in several gallons of whisky, with wine and tobacco. This supply was not paid for at the time, but the publican insisted on being paid out of the assets or being paid personally by the person who had ordered it. The poor farmer whose assets were to be so used would probably not have been able to get credit during his lifetime for a pint of whisky. I never allowed payment for this drink to be made when I could avoid it. The Roman Catholic clergy did much to discountenance the practice by insisting, when practicable, that the body should be brought into the church.

I was examined before Lord Peel's committee on the Licensing Acts, and told them what I have here written, and that the only way of putting a stop to wakes and their attendant crime would be to prevent the unlimited supply of drink on credit by making the cost of drink supplied at wakes irrecoverable, with the result that the amount ordered would be more in the shape of half-pints than gallons, as the publican would, of course, no longer give credit. The committee were divided on many points, but all sides agreed as to the advisability of adopting my suggestion.

I have always persistently opposed the granting of new licences except in very exceptional cases, and it is only fair to add that the instances in which landowners went astray as magistrates were very few and far between. During my thirty-one years I can only recollect two or three cases in which it occurred. On all other occasions they, and also the merchant · shopkeepers and large farmers who were magistrates, acted above reproach and beyond suspicion; but I had also to deal with a number of others who were always ready and willing at the beck and call of any intended publican or his canvassing friend, or a party convicted, to vote for a licence or for the reversal of a sentence on appeal. This was the class of magistrate I had principally to contend with.

Many eminent members of the Bar commenced their career before me in Kerry. The late Lord

Chancellor, Redmond Barry, was one of them. A young barrister, then known as Paddy Lynch, and now as Patrick Lynch, Esq., K.C., was another. The latter sat as deputy for me in the Midland Counties, and, I understand, gave universal satisfaction. Edward O'Farrell, now Sir Edward, the present Assistant Under-Secretary, also came before me, as also did Mr. Edward R. Wade, Legal Land Commissioner, Denis McCarthy Mahony, and the late William Hennessy, better known as the "Bard." While in Kerry I spent many pleasant evenings with the practitioners, some of whom sang very well.

The late Mr. Redmond Barry, afterwards Lord Chancellor, on one occasion was travelling through Kerry with some friends. When in Cahirciveen some of them became rather noisy in the hotel. Learning that they were going on to Mrs. Shea's hotel, which was some twenty miles away, and half-way to Killarney, the hotel proprietor wired her not to let the party in. When they arrived they found the door shut, and Mrs. Shea, the owner, point-blank refused them admittance. This was very hard on Redmond Barry, who had not taken the slightest part in the disturbance in Cahirciveen. He told this to Mrs. Shea, but she refused to yield, and the party had to go on the long drive to Killarney.

At the following Quarter Sessions Redmond Barry brought an action against Mrs. Shea for

failing to admit him in accordance with her duty as
an innkeeper. Mrs. Shea said she had been frightened at the receipt of the telegram, and, having no
man in the house, was afraid to admit the party. I
settled the matter by making Mrs. Shea say that
she was very sorry for refusing Mr. Barry, and
apologize to him in open court. And so the matter
ended. Patrick Lynch appeared as counsel for the
plaintiff.

Sir Edward Carson, then simply Edward Carson,
M.P., appeared on one occasion to prosecute Mr.
William O'Brien, who appealed before me from a
sentence of six months' imprisonment imposed on
him by the magistrates under the Crimes Act. He
was at the time undergoing a previous sentence of
six months. I was always opposed to imposing
sentences which were not concurrent. I spoke
strongly as to the illegality of Mr. O'Brien's
speeches, but, acting on my views, reduced the
sentence of six to four months' imprisonment, so as
to make it concurrent in termination with his
previous sentence.

Some years afterwards I was walking along the
riverside in Chamonix, when I came face to face
with Mr. and Mrs. O'Brien. I said: "Mr. O'Brien,
as old friends we can meet and talk on neutral
ground." We shook hands, and he introduced me
to Mrs. O'Brien, who seemed greatly amused when
she heard my name. After some conversation, I
said to him: "O'Brien, do you know what I have

been thinking." "No," he replied. I said : "If I served you rightly I should take you by the back of the neck and pitch you into that river." Both laughed, and from him at once came back the retort : "Well, Judge, let me say that is just what I was thinking I ought to do to you."

It is only right to add that Mr. O'Brien and I had been friends for many years. I knew him when he was on the staff of the *Freeman's Journal*, and had, as stated in my observations on the Dublin Mansion House Committee, in conjunction with my friend, Dr. Sigerson, obtained for him the writing of the report of the proceedings, a most able document, written with conspicuous fairness.

The most beautiful parts of the scenery in Kerry are comparatively unknown to the ordinary tourist. During my time in that county there was no railway communication with Cahirciveen, which is some forty-two miles distant from Killarney, and the railway to Dingle, some thirty miles beyond Tralee, had only just been finished a short time before I left. I remember travelling to Dingle on this line, our carriage being a railway-truck with a wooden rail round the edges, and chairs for our sitting accommodation. The line had not been finished, and we went off it several times during the trip. We, however, all arrived safely, and returned next day, having concluded the Sessions.

There could not be, in my opinion, a more

beautiful drive than that up Conor Hill, on the way to Dingle. As you ascend, you have in the valley to the east a splendid glimpse of the Killarney Lakes, and at the top of the stiff climb the "Windy Gap" opens out a grand view of Dingle Bay. It is truly distinctive in its beauty. The whole scene is charged with that delightful atmosphere of freshness characteristic of the west coast of Ireland.

My first appearance in Dingle was at the Revision Sessions, my wife being with me. We were met at the door of the hotel by a young woman, whose face was very red and swollen. She informed us that there was only one small bedroom and the coffee-room at our disposal. As I was not expected, the Judge's room was occupied by Major Hutchinson, the resident magistrate, who had gone off for the day with Mr. Gray, the District Inspector, and they were not expected home till late, so we had to put up with the scanty accommodation offered to us. I remember seeing a couple of bottles of Coleraine whisky on the Major's chimney-piece, while I had to imbibe some terrible stuff provided for us. During our visit we ascertained that the landlady was suffering from a bad attack of scarlet fever, so we were glad to leave the hotel. The R.M. afterwards proved most kind, and catered for us whenever we visited the town. Messrs. Gilbey had sent down a large stock of wine to their establishment in Dingle, and, among other wines, sent a stock of Madeira, which, not being a wine generally used by the inhabitants, had remained there for years until discovered by Major Hutchinson. During my time in Dingle I certainly helped to diminish the stock.

Happening one night to mention that I was fond of lemon-flavoured soda-water, the Major disappeared, and immediately reappeared with a most excellent bottle of that pleasant drink. The bottle was labelled " Made in Belfast." I remarked it was a long way from Belfast to Dingle. " No," he replied, " but it is a long way from Dingle to Belfast. It appeared that a merchant in the town, having the secret and good water, made large quantities of the soda-water, and as no one would buy lemon-flavoured soda-water made in such a place as Dingle, he labelled the bottles as " Made in Belfast." This he sold in large quantities throughout Ireland—even in Belfast—where the thirsty population drank it under the impression that they were encouraging local industry.

Dingle is a great fishing centre, but its people reap no direct food benefit from the fact as it is all sent straight off to London. The Major, however, managed to stop " in transitu " on one Friday a splendid turbot, which we all enjoyed together.

I remember on one occasion, when driving round the mountain-side towards Glenbeigh, remarking that, though on a very much smaller scale, the scenery did not suffer by comparison with Norway, which country I had just visited. The old mountain roads, going straight at every obstacle, and disdaining to skirt a mountain or hill, afforded me some splendid walks and opportunities of seeing the country.

I had to drive long distances during my time (1886-1891). Sitting up to eight o'clock, p.m., in Cahirciveen, I had often to drive the forty-two miles to Killarney, in order to sit in that town at ten o'clock next morning.

While sitting at Cahirciveen I frequently stayed at Waterville, ten miles distant, my hotel being beautifully situated on the shores of Lake Currawn. This lake is separated from the sea by a short river, which is about the earliest for salmon in Ireland, the fish running up early in January. It is a strange fact that a short distance higher up the coast there is a second river flowing into the sea, up which the salmon do not run till the month of July.

While at Waterville I made the acquaintance of Mr. Wilmot, the superintendent of the American telegraph line, which started from that place. He kindly showed me over the works. I was often astonished and interested to see the rapidity with which he could get a reply from New York, a fraction of a second only intervening between question and answer. There is a second line starting from Valentia, some miles away. On one occasion, passing through Cahirciveen on my way to

Waterville, I called at the post-office to send a telegram to the Waterville Hotel ordering dinner. To my astonishment, I was there informed that, though they could wire to New York or Dublin, there was no line to or from Waterville. While speaking to the postmaster on the subject, I saw Mr. Wilmot, and explained to him my difficulty. "Oh," said he, "I shall make that all right for you. Tell me the message you wish to have sent." I did as he requested. "Now," he added, "I shall send it on to New York through Valentia, with directions to have it sent back to Waterville on the other line." This he did, and I subsequently ascertained that Miss McElligott, the hotel-keeper, must have received the telegram a very short time after I had seen it sent off on its long journey to and from New York. Dinner was ready at Waterville when I arrived.

While in Kerry I had to deal with the Land League as a proclaimed, and consequently an illegal, society. Very many meetings of the body were, however, surreptitiously held in that county. It was very difficult to obtain evidence as to what was taking place or being discussed at any assembly of the League, the members of which became very loyal and law-abiding on the approach of a constable.

In one case which came before me on appeal the police succeeded in proving their case in an amusing manner. It became known to the police authorities that a fully attended meeting was to be held in a valley surrounded by high hills, not far from Killarney. Sentinels were stationed on the hilltops to give warning as to the approach of the police. Two young constables, stretched at full length, crawled up the side of the hill unseen by the sentinels. When at the top they had a full view of the meeting and the parties who were there. Their sudden appearance as they stood up literally put the meeting to flight. Horses were mounted and whipped into headlong flight, cars were filled and driven away nearly as rapidly, and when the constables arrived on the scene not a man was visible.

But, unfortunately for the members, their secretary left behind him in his perturbation and hurry the minute-book, containing the names of all who were present, the resolutions passed, and full particulars. These, of course, were not intended for publication.

CHAPTER XXVIII

JUDICIAL WORK IN KERRY

UNDER the Irish Land Law tenants, in applying to have a fair rent fixed, had the option of selecting one of two tribunals. They could either apply to the County Court Judge, who was assisted by a Court valuer, paid by the Government, or to the Head Land Commission, who sent it for hearing to three sub-commissioners, one legal and two lay, there being an appeal from both tribunals to the Head Commission.

The tenants, as might have been expected, having regard to the exorbitant rents they had been paying on many estates, made applications in great numbers. Very many of them came in before me in Kerry and the four Midland Counties, and I fixed fair rents in hundreds of cases, giving substantial reductions, to which I considered they were entitled. But gradually the landlords became dissatisfied with the amount of my reductions, being of opinion that they were too large, and of late years removed nearly all cases from my court to the Head Commission, who sent them on to be tried by the sub-commissioners. This course was open to the landlord, owing to the provisions of the Act, and the opposition of the tenants was not allowed to prevail. These facts also sufficiently prove that, notwithstanding writings and speeches, the tenants of those counties as a body reposed full confidence in my action in their regard.

During my lengthened career as Judge for five years in the County Kerry, and twenty-six years in the Midland Counties of Longford, Meath, Westmeath, and King's, I have had some pleasant, and also some very unpleasant, experiences. It was always a source of great pleasure to me to meet my officers and practitioners on my quarterly visits. The great bulk of the population in the several counties was, I knew, satisfied, feeling that what I did was for their protection and benefit.

I never objected to agitation for the redressing of real grievances, provided that agitation were confined within legal bounds ; but all through those thirty-one years after I had concluded the investigation into the Phœnix Park murders, I had, in support of law and order, to deal with a number of men who, perhaps having what they considered a good object in view, insisted on attaining it by the use of the illegal means to which I have already referred.

For some time during my stay in Kerry that county was, as I have said, in a very disturbed state. It had been visited by Joseph Brady, a leading member of the Invincibles, who spent some time working at Ballyseedy, a place some eight miles from Castleisland, with the result that the Moonlighters increased in number, and became very dangerous to those who were anxious to live peaceably with their neighbours and remain law-abiding citizens. Murders became frequent, and generally took place on Saturday nights. So accustomed were the inhabitants to their constant recurrence, that the question on Sunday morning was not, " Was there a murder last night ?" but simply, " Where was it last night ?"

I had also in that county, as I have said, to deal with the members of the suppressed Land League, who persisted, notwithstanding the law, in holding their meetings and denouncing any persons whom they considered unfriendly to their cause.

A Kerryman can tell a lie as well as any man, but my experience of them has been that their lies are easily seen through and detected. A case came before me in which a man was charged with posting a threatening notice denouncing certain individuals. He was found by the police in a room in which were a number of other men. A witness was produced for the defence who swore the prisoner was there for the innocent purpose of cutting their hair, and the scissors he used was produced. I asked the witness if he had seen the prisoner use the scissors. He replied in the affirmative. I had remarked that the paper produced by the police, taken from the place to which it had been affixed, had the four corners cleanly cut off; so, taking the paper in my hands, and imitating with my first and second fingers the action of a scissors, I proceeded to pretend to cut my hair and then to cut off the four corners of the paper, asking him on his oath to deny that that was what the prisoner did. He was so astonished at my action, suggesting, as it did, what had actually occurred, that he collapsed, and could say nothing more, and I confirmed the conviction of the magistrates.

In writing of the propensity and ability of the Kerryman for lying, I do not wish in the slightest degree to detract from the powers in that line of some of those in the Midland Counties, who in safe all-round hard swearing could leave the first-named far behind.

A large shopkeeper in one of the Midland towns died, leaving a considerable number of debts, which were secured by promissory notes. At one Sessions I had before me a large batch of civil bills brought by his executors to recover the amounts of the notes. One witness deposed to seeing each of the defendants sign the notes, and a second witness swore to their handwriting. Each defendant as he was sworn denied positively that it was his handwriting. I told the first who did so that I should send him for trial for perjury, and after I had dealt in a similar manner with some dozen of them, the Crown Solicitor begged of me to cease, as other-wise I should have nearly the entire district in custody. I saw the difficulty, and then announced that I should adjourn all the cases till next Sessions, and that I should then certainly send for trial all those who persisted in their denial. When next I sat I was informed that I should not be further troubled, as the defendants had all paid. I may add such a defence is frequent in suits brought by the executors of a deceased trader.

In one case I had sentenced a man, convicted before me of perjury, to six months' imprisonment. At the end of the fourth month of his sentence I willingly agreed to his discharge by His Excellency, as I considered that, while in prison he was only a memory, he was when moving again amongst his friends and neighbours—a reminder—an outward and visible testimony to the danger of committing perjury.

I found when I first went to Kerry that one of the main causes—if not the main cause—of that county being in such a disturbed and lawless state was the endeavour by many landlords to insist on the payment by the tenants of the arrears due, which at the time amounted to a very considerable sum. I saw that there would be no peace in the county as long as these arrears were insisted on. I gradually got the consent of many of the landlords that I should deal with them, and, acting fairly between the two, I struck out a very large amount of the arrears, and obtained for the landlords a portion of the rents which they had not been receiving for years. In cases where the landlords did not consent I endorsed on the decree that it was not to be executed as long as the tenant paid the instalments made by me—instalments which I thought he could pay in addition to the accruing rent. This course was held to be illegal. Nevertheless, such an endorsement was afterwards legalized by an Act passed in the year 1887, and the Council of County Court Judges, in framing the Rules of 1890 under that Act, adopted the endorsement and words used by me which had been decided to be illegal.

There were in Kerry a number of insolvent estates with only nominal landlords, which were under the jurisdiction of the Receiver Judge, then Mr. Justice Boyd. I investigated each case and found arrears had been allowed to increase to a considerable extent, and that having regard to the poverty of the tenant, they were quite irrecoverable. In all such cases I so marked them and struck them out. The Receiver Judge wrote, remonstrating with me as interfering with his jurisdiction ; but I replied that I had a far better opportunity of judging of the merits of each case than he had, as I could personally examine both tenant and agent, whereas the Receiver Judge had to depend upon the *ex parte* statement of the Receiver.

It may be that I adopted strong measures in that

county in dealing with both landlord and tenant, but Sir Michael Hicks-Beach, afterwards Lord St. Aldwyn, in a case before the Dublin Magistrates where he was examined as a witness, described and approved of my action as "compulsion within the law." Whatever may have been the means, the result was most satisfactory. The tenants for whom I did my best were satisfied ; and, that the landlords were also pleased is evidenced by the address presented by them to me, to which I have already referred.

The following cases will illustrate my course of action and the difficulties I had to contend with in Kerry : In one case an extensive landowner brought ejectments before me against a considerable number of his tenants, who had persistently refused to pay any rent unless all the arrears—which amounted to a large sum—had been forgiven. The ejectments were the result of a threat on their part to put into operation the " Plan of Campaign," then rampant in the county. I asked the solicitor for plaintiff if he could remit any of the arrears or allow me to deal with them. He refused to do either, saying that he had received a letter from his principal that morning stating he was to obtain decrees in every case where the arrears had not been paid up. He handed me this letter of instruction to read. I read it, and, giving it back to him, asked him if he had read the postscript on the other side of the page. He replied he had not seen it, and was very much astonished on reading it to find a direction to him to inform me that the writer, notwithstanding the earlier part of his letter, wished to leave the entire discretion to deal with the arrears in my hands. I accordingly said I should do so. I then called before me the bailiff on the estate—a very fair-minded man—and, going seriatim into the case of all the tenants, ascertained from him what amount each could pay at once, and how much, if any, of the arrears he could also pay. I considered his evidence just and fair, and adjourned all the cases for a week, intimating that I should do my best for all those who complied with the terms and brought into court the sum fixed by me on the bailiff's evidence.

On the following week all without exception brought the amount named by me, and a very considerable sum was received by the agent and solicitor, who said it was the best collection they had had for some time, and that no rents had been paid for many years ; and, as a further result of my action, the incubus of arrears no longer worried the tenants, and the " Plan of Campaign " was foiled.

In another case, while the " Plan " was in its full force in the county, and the tenants were ordered to lodge their rents in the War Chest, I dealt in the same manner with the tenants of an impoverished owner, but gave them at their request till my next Quarter Sessions to pay the instalments fixed by me.

In the meantime a meeting of the League was held in the immediate neighbourhood, and the tenants were denounced for agreeing to my terms, and ordered to join with the other tenants in Ireland who had adopted the "Plan of Campaign." The result was that, when I sat at the next Quarter Sessions, not a single tenant came before me. As I pitied their trouble, and felt that they had been afraid to come in, I further adjourned the cases. When I again sat they all appeared in court, and begged me to give them the same terms, saying that they had been afraid to enter the court the previous Sessions. I was very glad to be able to do so, and, the tenants having paid the amount I fixed, I struck off the bulk of the arrears, and they went away rejoicing.

The house of a respectable farmer named Curtin was attacked at night by a number of Moonlighters, who demanded his firearms. He refused to give them up, and as they seemed determined to proceed to extremities, and were all armed and disguised, he in self-defence and in defence of his wife and family fired and shot dead one of them. Another of them fired and killed Curtin himself. Mrs. Curtin, instead of having sympathy extended to her, was boycotted by a number of the neighbours to an alarming extent, and her workmen all left her employment, many of them through fear. Five or six men were convicted and sentenced to imprisonment by the magistrates.

I had no difficulty in confirming the conviction. The charge against them was that they had been instrumental in getting up the boycott against Mrs. Curtin, and had prevented men working for her. I adjourned the question of sentence till next morning. When I had retired to my chamber Mrs. Curtin came in to me, and implored me to let off one of the men, who—she told me—though one of the boycotters, had come by night to work for her. I said I should consider the matter, and, if possible, not punish him. Next morning I saw the Head Constable, and told him what Mrs. Curtin had said. "For God's sake, sir," said the Head, "don't discharge him. They already suspect him, and he would be shot to-morrow if he was liberated to-day." So I had to send the poor fellow for his own protection to prison with the other men.

One other case will illustrate a further change in the law brought about by my action in Kerry—a change which was most beneficial to tenants. In the Famine Year, 1847, the late Lord Lansdowne, a very large landowner in that county, refrained from collecting, but did not remit, a year's rent, which he left still due by the tenants. The result of this was that, though the tenants continued to pay their rents regularly, their receipts were all dated as of the year before, and consequently, though paying, as they thought, up to the last gale-day, according to the receipt one year's rent was still owing.

There could be no better or kinder landlord than the present Lord Lansdowne, who continued the system; but I considered that in the hands of another landlord, who might be unscrupulous, such an arrangement would work unfairly to tenants, as, notwithstanding their punctual payments for years, they were always liable to be evicted on the ground that one year's rent was in arrear, this being evidenced by the receipt accepted by the tenant. When I first had any of Lord Lansdowne's ejectments before me, I found he only claimed rent up to twelve months preceding the last gale-day before action. I refused to give decrees unless the date of the last gale of the current year were included, so as to free the tenant from the year's rent carried forward for so many years, and said it should be inserted in place of rent alleged to be due the year before. The same rule applied to tenants of ordinary holdings, all of whom—even those who had recently become tenants—had their rents receipted a year back.

A lengthy correspondence between Lord Lansdowne, the agent, and myself took place. His Excellency, then Governor-General of Canada, wrote to his agent—Mr. Trench—with directions to inform me as to the reasons for his action; but I could see no reason for keeping hanging over the tenants' heads a year's rent which could not have been paid in the Famine Year, and I still refused to grant decrees unless the change were made. My dear friend the late David Mahony argued strongly that he was entitled to his decrees under the words of the then existing law; but I held my view. The law, I knew, was doubtful; but very soon afterwards it was made clear by an Act passed in the year 1896.

At present a landlord must include in his ejectment the last gale of the current year immediately preceding the bringing of the action.

The Royal Irish Constabulary are a splendid body of men, and in the past troublesome times in Ireland their duties in support of law and order, which were most arduous, were performed in a most efficient manner, notwithstanding the fact that they were as a rule recruited from the labouring and small farmer class, and imbued with the opinions and sympathies of that section of the community. His Majesty has at the present time no more loyal subjects than the members of the Royal Irish Constabulary—as witness the number of them who have left the force to join the army and fight our country's battle.

Their loyalty was brought forcibly to my mind by the following incident while I was sitting in Killarney : The men were in the habit of spending any spare time boating on the lake. One afternoon the District Inspector, Mr. Rogers, invited me to go with him and the men for a row on the lake. I, of course, consented. The boat was an eight-oared one, and the eight men formed a splendid group, headed by a Sergeant, whom I was delighted afterwards to meet as District Inspector in one of my counties. We had also with us a ninth constable, who played the cornopian. After some time we saw that we were being followed by a large boat filled with a number of local men and "returned Americans." On seeing that I was in the constabulary boat, they commenced to boo and shout defiantly. Suddenly the cornopian in our boat played out "God save the Queen," and the eight oarsmen lustily joined in and shouted the words, to the astonishment, and no doubt disgust, of the other boat's crew, who ceased their defiant attitude and departed.

After my change to Kerry in the year 1886, I was succeeded in the position of County Court Judge and Chairman of Quarter Sessions in the four Midland Counties—Meath, Westmeath, King's County, and Longford—by the Hon. Gerald Fitzgerald, who had occupied a similar position in the counties of Sligo and Roscommon, Judge O'Connor Morris going to those two counties in his place. Judge Fitzgerald was appointed Judicial Land Commissioner in the year 1890, and was succeeded in the Midland Counties by the late Judge Hickson, on whose death in 1891 I returned to my former position in the four Midland Counties, and held that post until I retired in January, 1914. The late Judge Shaw, afterwards Recorder of Belfast, took my place in Kerry.

CHAPTER XXIX

MIDLAND COUNTIES—BOYCOTTING

I RETURNED to the Midland Counties from Kerry in 1891. Notwithstanding the operation of the Crimes Act, agrarian agitation, with its resultant trail of crime, was very rife; and in these counties I had to commence again the fight for peace and law and order which I had just concluded in Kerry. To put it mildly, I was not popular, and when it became necessary in the course of my duty to confirm convictions under the Crimes Act in Longford against Mr. J. P. Farrell, M.P., and in King's County against Messrs. Haviland Burke, Reddy, and others, I incurred the most violent hostility. I was subjected to torrents of abuse, verbal and written, in all the four counties. Nevertheless, the Crimes Act effected its purpose. The terror of its penalties restrained even the most lawless, and the long and lamentable catalogue of agrarian crimes was greatly diminished. It seemed, indeed, that peace was in sight at last. But it was not yet to be, for the dropping of the Crimes Act about the time of the change of Government in 1905 permitted of the revival with impunity of most of the old evils, and Irish affairs were again put back into a " seething pot." Boycotting increased to an alarming extent in Longford and Westmeath, and to a less extent in King's County and Meath. Malicious fires and injuries became frequent in all four counties, especially in Meath and Westmeath. Cattle-driving, which commenced in Westmeath, soon extended to Meath, and increased day by day. It at length attained to such immense proportions that I had fifty cases of this class of offence to deal with from one Sessions to another in the County Meath.

In the case of malicious injuries and cattle-drives I gave liberal compensation to be paid out of the rates, and so after some years put a stop to them, the neighbours of the injured party realizing that the game was not a paying one.

The Act of Parliament enabling a Judge in my position to give compensation has been variously discussed. It has been said that it is unfair to make the innocent pay for the acts of others. Granting this view to have some foundation, it must be remembered that very many of the rate-payers, if not parties to the acts, were, at least to a very considerable extent, sympathizers with the offenders, and if they did not sympathize, would probably do their best to stop the acts complained of, and if not able to do anything else, could at least denounce them. From another point of view

the law may be looked upon as an insurance for
innocent parties.   The amount payable by the individual ratepayer for malicious injuries is not considerable, and a party who entertains ill-feeling or
spite against his innocent neighbour will be less
anxious or liable to injure his property if aware that
the burthen of the loss would not be that neighbour's, but would fall on the district at large.   In
this way I was able to compensate those whose property had been in any way maliciously injured.

The procedure adopted by the Crown would never
have put down cattle-driving.   Sending the guilty
parties to prison for a month in default of giving
bail was quite futile.   Those men went in as
martyrs and came out as heroes, but the parties
whose property was interfered with had some
redress; I gave, as I have said, compensation for
their losses, payable out of the rates.

It was different in the case of boycotting, which
was openly advocated in Longford and Westmeath
by Members of Parliament and other leaders.   Time
after time in my charges to the Grand Juries I
called the attention of the Government to the
desperate position of those boycotted.   To one
realizing as I did their dire plight, it was incom-
prehensible that, with the exception of a couple
of prosecutions at Assizes, in which no person ever
anticipated a jury would agree, a strong Government held out no helping hand to any of them.

The boycotting which reappeared was of a most

16

virulent description, and was again openly advocated by the same parties. I could do nothing to
help the unfortunate people who were being boycotted beyond calling the attention of the public to
their deplorable position.

In Westmeath a gentleman was boycotted to
such an extent that his Catholic female servants
were attacked on Sundays as they left the church
where they had been hearing Mass. I had to
break the licence of the shopkeeper and publican
who refused to supply that gentleman with
goods.

It was much worse in Longford. There an
influential Member of Parliament lent the aid of
his powerful local newspaper to urge on the hunting
down of the unfortunate persons who were the subject of the boycott. I was myself, time after time,
denounced in its columns in the strongest language
for my action in the matter. The extraordinary
and cruel boycotting of the Messrs. McCann and of
their servants, and of all those who dared the powers
that were rampant for many years in Longford and
Westmeath, are too well known for repetition
here. Many of those who used strong language
against landowners and boycotted persons, I knew,
never intended or considered that their language might lead to malicious injuries. But they
should have reflected that men going home full of
patriotism and whisky might consider that they
were fully complying with the fervid oratory they

had just been listening to if, when passing the barn of an obnoxious party, they took advantage of the darkness to set it on fire.

A threat of the Crimes Act would have saved all these poor people years of miserable existence ; but nothing beyond stationing a few policemen in the houses or patrolling the neighbourhood was ever done to help them in their desperate plight, except a couple of prosecutions, which, as I have said, everyone knew would fail.

It is true, they made a martyr of Mr. Farrell by sending him to jail in default of bail, which, of course, resulted in a second big collection being made throughout the country for him. This action did not put a stop to boycotting. The evil continued as pronouncedly as ever for several years, when gradually the boycotter became sick of his practices, and it partially died out. Then at last the unfortunate people who had suffered untold misery simply because they had asserted their right to deal with their property according as the law allowed them, and had been left by the Government practically to shift for themselves, began to breathe freely again.

CHAPTER XXX

JUDICIAL WORK IN LONGFORD AND MEATH

HAVING regard to speeches and the writings in the local Press, and that of some of the adjoining counties, I looked upon myself as the most unpopular man in the County Longford. That this was not so, and that my unpopularity was confined to those who had nothing to lose, or who sympathized with the bad work going on, became apparent to me in the following pleasant manner: I had been invited by my friend Monsignor O'Farrell, P.P., of Ardagh, a very pretty village distant some miles from Longford, to be present at the consecration of his beautiful church. Cardinal Logue and several prelates also attended, including the Most Rev. Dr. Hoare, who takes one of his titles from that village.

At the luncheon after the ceremony a large concourse of people from the surrounding district and the town of Longford were present. At that time I considered that on account of my action my unpopularity was at its zenith, and looked forward with fear and trembling to the reception I should receive when responding to the toast of my name, proposed by Monsignor O'Farrell. Cardinal Logue, who spoke before my turn came, was received, as might be expected, by the assembly with enthusiastic applause. What was, then, my astonishment when I stood up to find myself greeted with applause as enthusiastic as, if not more enthusiastic than, that accorded to His Eminence; and, when the cheers had subsided, I was greatly flattered by hearing a voice which I thought I recognized as that of my friend the chairman of the Longford Branch of the United Irish League, calling for three cheers more for Judge Curran, a call which was heartily responded to. Afterwards, when mixing through the crowd, I had many a friendly shake hands. I did not consider their warm greeting as showing that they agreed altogether with my action or language in dealing with the state of the country, but simply as an indication that they appreciated my intentions. I may here state that for over forty years I have been honoured by the personal friendship of His Eminence.

How well I was entitled to use strong language as to the state of lawlessness and crime which existed at the time in the four counties will become apparent from the following occurrences and the figures of the sums awarded by me for malicious injuries during the twelve years before my retirement. I am happy to say matters have greatly improved, and the old system of crime and outrage is fast becoming a "negligible quantity." I do not intend now to repeat what I have said about boycotting, to whose victims, unless it was followed by crime, I could afford no remedy.

In the County Longford, where boycotting was in its worst form, and a number of individuals had to receive constant personal protection, and the farms of others had to be constantly patrolled by police, I had to award during those years the sum of £1,394 as compensation to the sufferers from malicious injuries, including the sum of £1,178, for the malicious burning of dwelling-houses, barns, hay, etc.

Cattle-driving never proved a success in the County Longford. The first attempt proved an utter failure, owing to the energetic action of a body of the Royal Irish Constabulary, under the command of the District Inspector, Mr. George Hurst, now County Inspector in the County Mayo. It was announced by the leaders of the local branches of the United Irish League that a demonstration in force would be held on the road bordering the lands of the Messrs. McCann, to whose case I have already referred. The meeting was called for the purpose of demonstrating the disapproval by the League of the action of those gentlemen in taking land under the eleven months' system for grazing purposes. A large number of persons sympathizing with the object of the League attended, and eventually many of them, obeying what they deemed the suggestion of the various leaders, broke into the land with the avowed intention of driving off the cattle. They were, however, followed by Mr. Hurst and his force of men, and scattered in all directions, leaving the lands much more quickly than they had entered them. After that fiasco cattle-driving disappeared from the county.

The Messrs. McCann afterwards brought an action for trespass against those who had entered their lands, and I awarded decrees of £5, and costs against each. They were many in number, and counsel for the defendants made the point that, as it was a joint action, there could only be one decree ; but, as in the case of Mr. Craddock and the Ormonde Hunt, I held that each trespasser was responsible for his own acts, and Lord Justice Holmes, who heard the appeals taken from my decrees, held that I was right and affirmed them all.

A very usual practice in all four counties, having for its object the prevention of the sale of cattle by boycotted persons, was to cut off the animals' tails. Whether this was done by cutting the tail off altogether, as was the case in many instances, or simply by cutting off the hairs at the end of the tail, the result was the same : the animal became unsaleable either privately or in the public market. No one would buy it. A purchaser would not himself be able to sell any cattle so treated, as the mere possession of them would point him out as a boycotted person, as one who had disobeyed the orders of the League.

Boycotting, incendiary fires, and other injuries were the result frequently of private animosity, and not of agrarian agitation. The parties, taught by experience, had a ready weapon at hand. In the County Meath a Mrs. Mary Carley, who lived with her two sisters in a house in a lonely district, had displeased some of her neighbours. The result was that in the year 1910 a portion of her house and her hay was maliciously burned, and I had to award her the sum of £128. During the hearing of the case I was informed that more of her property had been burned while she was in court before me, including what had been left of her house by the first burning. The next Sessions she came again before me. It then appeared in evidence that while she was absent proving her case at the previous Sessions, the remainder of her house and hay, to the value of £30, had been burned, which amount I had to award. The burning was not the result of any agrarian agitation, but of private enmity and for the purpose of revenge.

In the County Meath during the same period I had to award the large amount of £6,241, to be paid out of the rates, to those who had been the objects of malicious injuries. This amount included the sum of £4,640 for the malicious burning of dwelling-houses, stables, lofts, barns, hay, straw, and oats; it also included the sum of £396 for cattle-driving.

Meath is essentially a grazing county, the land not being very suitable for tillage. As a result, there were in it a large number of grazing-farms suitable and used for fattening cattle to be sold in the Dublin and English markets. I considered it a very short-sighted and selfish policy on the part of the small Meath farmers to object to this use of the lands, as the owners of small farms in the remainder of Ireland had no land sufficiently good to fatten the cattle reared by them except helped by the Irish or English proprietors of large tracts of grass-land upon which the cattle of these men could be rendered fit for market; and the shutting off of the Irish grazier would leave the small farmer at the mercy of English purchasers, who, in default of competition, could name their own prices.

It was asserted that the grazing-lands should be divided among small men, and so a wicked crusade against all graziers began. A large grazier in the county named William Dove, whose residence was close to the County Westmeath, appeared before me in the year 1908 claiming compensation for the malicious burning of cattle-sheds, with corn-lofts, 1 hay-barn, 200 tons of hay, 50 barrels of rye, 100 barrels of oats, 13 head of fat cattle, and other property. He was a large employer of labour, much respected, and very well liked in the district, and on terms of friendship with all his neighbours. But these facts went for nothing; the "ban" of the grazier was on him, and one night all the above property was maliciously set on fire and destroyed. I awarded Mr. Dove the sum of £1,370 and costs, which sum represented in only a small degree his real loss. As he lived within one mile of the County Westmeath, I put the sum of £600 and a share of the costs on that county. The Westmeath District Council appealed, with the result that the Judge of Assize affirmed my decree as to the total amount, but varied it by making County Westmeath pay one-half of the amount decreed by me, with costs. As a matter of fact, the appeal was rather a failure.

In the year 1914 I had to award against the same county the sum of £1,000 for the malicious burning of a large building, including a quantity of machinery, the property of Mr. Christopher Daly.

These amounts may seem large, but, as a matter of fact, in such cases I always kept well within the mark, and at one Assizes the Lord Chief Baron complained that my awards were not large enough, and in one case, in affirming my decree, he increased the amount; and in another case the late Mr. Justice Wright added £200 to £600 awarded by me in the King's County for the malicious burning of stables, in which were a number of valuable horses. The decree was afterwards, upon a case stated by the learned Judge as to the sufficiency of the notices served under the Act, reversed by the Court of Appeal.

It is very pleasant now for me to reflect that, after so many years of great anxiety in combating the result of illegal agitation, I should, on my retirement in 1914, have left the four Midland Counties comparatively free from crime.

Through the kindness of my friend, Mr. George Knight, Clerk of the Crown and Peace for the County Meath, I am enabled to give my readers some figures which show the state of that county sixty years ago. It is interesting to compare them with the present and the late state of Meath. During late years there has been very little ordinary crime in the four counties, the crime being, as I have shown, to a considerable extent the result of misguided and unlawful agitation. At the Trim Lenten Assizes for the year 1818 there were 58 bills sent before the Grand Jury against 108 prisoners. The cases numbered nearly every offence known to the law, including murder. At the Summer Assizes for the same year there were 62 bills sent to the Grand Jury against 89 prisoners for the same class of offence. At the Lenten Assizes of 1828 there were 44 bills against 77 prisoners, the cases being of a similar class, with some bad additions. At the

Summer Assizes of 1828 there were 52 bills against 80 prisoners, with the addition of highway robbery and other offences. At the Lenten Assizes of 1838 there were 40 bills sent up against 61 prisoners, and that year Whiteboyism appears for the first time as an offence. In the year 1848 there were 52 bills against 79 prisoners. At the Summer Assizes there were 21 bills and 24 prisoners. Stealing food seems to have been a very common offence in this year— the year of the famine.

From that time matters somewhat improved, until ordinary crime became very much less, and the crime of later years, to which I have referred, took its place.

In a case tried before me in Trim I was very much impressed by the great ability of the late Lord Justice Moriarty. A young scion of a county family, on the last night of his holidays, determined to have a "rare old time," and, having collected the servants, headed by the butler, and led by himself, they proceeded during the night to awaken all the neighbours, frightening some of them considerably. One, however, did not see any joke in the matter, and stoutly resisted the intrusion, being under the impression that they intended to attack his house, with the result that an assault took place. The police arrived on the scene, and they were all returned for trial before me.

Considering the agitation against landowners

which then existed in the county, it was a very difficult case to defend before a jury of farmers; but Sergeant Moriarty, as he then was, turned the entire case into such ridicule that it was, I might say, laughed out of court.

CHAPTER XXXI

KING'S COUNTY—ORMONDE HUNT

In the King's County during the same period the sum awarded by me for malicious injuries amounted to the large figure of £4,333, including the following: Burning dwelling-houses, barns, etc., £998; hay, straw, etc., £893; maiming cattle, £178; cattle-driving, £130.

Cattle-maiming was of rather frequent, too frequent, occurrence in the King's County. At one sitting in Birr, in the year 1908, I had before me several such cases. They were applications for compensation for malicious injury. In one case I had to award a farmer named Guinan the sum of £10, the injury being the cutting clean off of the hind-leg of his foal. In another case I awarded £5 to a farmer for injuries to an eight-year-old mare. The shoulder was injured, and the animal's two fore-legs had been cut over the knee. In two other cases I had to award substantial compensation for the maiming of cattle by cutting off their tails—some completely, some partially—and other injuries, the object of this nefarious practice being, as I have stated, to injure the owners by preventing the sale of the animals by marking them as boycotted. When pronouncing my awards I said " I was unable to find language strong enough to express my feelings regarding such savagery. The man who did the act dared not attack a man in the open, but, instead, vented his fury on the poor brute, which could not defend itself. The advocates of cattle-driving and mob violence were morally responsible for such outrages."

At Birr, King's County, in the month of January, 1908, I had before me several very disgraceful, and, to the district, discreditable cases, arising out of the stoppage of the Ormonde Hunt Club.

Hunting in Ireland has always been looked upon as a great national pastime. It was not only a source of pleasure to the members of the several clubs, but also a source of emolument and profit to those in the district who were farmers, horse-dealers, hotel-keepers, and that large body of labourers and servants who are concerned in the management and care of horses.

The Ormonde Hunt Club in the King's County, composed of local gentlemen, fulfilled all these conditions, and all its members were on terms of friendship with the farmers over whose lands the Hunt was in the habit of riding. Two of its members—brothers named Kenny, sons of a local magistrate—had prosecuted some men for cattle-driving ; but the charge had been dismissed by a majority of the magistrates, who held the extraordinary doctrine that cattle-driving was not a criminal offence. The Shinrone branch of the United Irish League immediately passed a resolution demanding from the club the expulsion of the Messrs. Kenny, and calling upon farmers not to allow members of the club to ride over their lands until that event had taken place.

The secretary of the club wrote saying that the Messrs. Kenny did not intend for the present to hunt with the Ormondes. The secretary of the League replied, saying that nothing but their expulsion would satisfy the League. In the meantime, and before he was aware of this last letter, Mr. Craddock, Master of the Hounds, being under the impression that every matter had been satisfactorily arranged, sent out his fixture card calling a meet of the hounds to be held at his house on the following Monday. Mr. Rolleston, the club secretary, also wrote, saying there would not be time to bring the further communication before the committee till after the following Monday.

A special meeting of the League body was held on the Sunday, and a resolution passed that, as the Hunt Committee had not agreed to their terms, hunting should be stopped by force. During the afternoon the following manifesto was spread broadcast in the district: "Stop the Hunt! The Ormonde Club have published fixtures in defiance of the Shinrone U.I.L., and in violation of the terms of their own letter. They back the graziers against the people. The men of Shinrone and Ballingarry are fighting the people's fight. They ask all Nationalists to support them. Come in your thousands to Fairy Hill on Monday at ten o'clock. Teach insolent men a lesson. Stop the Hunt!"

The result was what might be expected. On the Monday morning a crowd of several hundred men, armed with sticks and bottles, including a local M.P., and, headed by a brass band, went to Mr. Thomas Craddock's residence, where a considerable number of the Hunt Club had assembled. The crowd behaved in a most disorderly manner, breaking into and greatly damaging the pleasure grounds, and threatening with assault all who opposed them. On a subsequent day a similar attack was made at the residence of a gentleman named Whitfield, where two of the dogs were injured, and many persons were attacked by the same gang. Several of these latter were sued in damages by Mr. Craddock and Mr. Whitfield before me, and in the result I made them pay dearly for their action.

By consent I tried the cases of Mr. Craddock and Mr. Whitfield together, and I awarded £20 against each of four of the defendants, including the secretary of the Shinrone League, and awarded the sum of £15 against each of eight defendants, and £5 against one.

17

Mr. Craddock, who was paid £700 as Master of the Hounds, lost his position, and the Ormonde Hunt Club was broken up; and the advantage of the resulting expenditure was lost to the district. I gave those who were the cause of the disruption reason to remember the part they played in it for many a day.

Two of the defendants, including the M.P., lived in the County Tipperary, but I was informed they fared very badly before my friend Judge Moore.

I told the defendants that I could not allow mob law to prevail, and that the law of the land was superior to that of the Shinrone League. I may add that the above sums did not include costs, which were very heavy.

These cases had a remarkable and somewhat startling sequel. In the month of March following the issuing of the decrees the Sheriff seized under them some twenty head of cattle, the property of several of the defendants, and placed them apparently secure in the pound in Birr, where they were to remain some two or three days prior to their sale by the Sheriff. Every precaution had been taken to safeguard them. The cattle could not escape except by the gate, which was securely fastened by the head bailiff, and day and night the place was under the supervision of bailiffs and the police. But notwithstanding all these precautions, it was found one morning that the cattle had all disappeared during the previous night. The most exacting inquiries failed to discover how and when the animals were spirited away. They were, however, recaptured by the police on a farm a considerable distance off, and sold by the Sheriff next day. Many of them were bought in by their owners.

I had before me some years ago a case of what is known as "ragging." Some of the young officers of a militia regiment, stationed in Birr, disapproving of what they considered bad form on the part of an officer, broke into his house at night, searching, without avail, for him. They eventually had to leave without having attained their object. They were arrested, and sent for trial before me. George Wright (afterwards Mr. Justice Wright) defended them. They were all sons or relatives of local and county gentlemen. The jury, without hesitation, acquitted them.

The case for the Crown came to grief, as the prosecutor remained locked up in his room during the time the defendants were in the house, and failed to identify them. On being asked what kept him in his room for such a long time, he replied he was searching for his trousers, and could not find them in the dark—a statement which gave rise to an observation in court: "Surely a Highlander would have found his breeches in the time."

Though from time to time during the worst state of the agitation I had in court to use strong language denouncing the action of many Members of Parliament and others who composed the body of the United Irish League, our outside intercourse was in many cases of a very friendly nature.

During the hearing of the trial of Mr. Parnell and others I had many opportunities of meeting Michael Davitt and knowing and appreciating his upright character and his honest desire to carry on the agitation without crime. I met him one day some years after I had felt myself bound to affirm convictions against some of the leaders of his party. After the usual greeting, I said to him : " It is a long time, Mr. Davitt, since we have met." " Quite so, but I think that is all the better for me," was his good-humoured rejoinder.

I had a somewhat peculiar meeting with Mr. Edward Harrington, M.P., in Kerry. On one occasion, travelling from Tralee to Dublin, I found that I had that gentleman as a fellow-passenger on the same train. He had been sentenced to a term of imprisonment under the Crimes Act, and was being conveyed in custody from Tralee to Dublin. I got out of the train to have a cup of tea at Mallow. While enjoying it I looked round and saw Mr. Harrington at my side, also having a cup. I had known him for some time, and after a few words of conversation with him I gave the attendant a shilling, out of which I intended that she should take sixpence, the price of my tea. Seeing that I appeared to be a friend of Mr. Harrington, she said : " Is this for the tea of both ?" I found myself unable to be ungenerous enough to say I would not give Mr. Harrington a cup of tea, so I said yes. At the same time the jailer came forward to say he had the money to pay. However, I paid for the tea, and left the matter so. Shortly afterwards I read in a local, and also in a Dublin paper, a paragraph headed " Judge Curran invites Mr. Harrington, M.P., to tea while in custody."

Under this head I may also include my meeting with Mr. William O'Brien in Switzerland, already referred to.

Under the Crimes Act the addition of hard labour to a sentence of imprisonment had the result of incapacitating the party convicted from holding any public appointment or office for a term of five years.

I suggested to Mr. Farrell, member for North Longford, when charged before me, that I should remit the imprisonment imposed upon him by the magistrates if he would consent to give up his advocacy of boycotting and cease the publication in his paper of a number of threatening resolutions passed by a set of nobodies in the branches of the United Irish League. To this course Mr. Farrell positively refused to consent, and for this reason I had to leave the addition of " hard labour " in his sentence.

However, matters quietened down very considerably, and boycotting became very much lessened until it again revived as already stated. Shortly afterwards, in the hope that things had permanently improved—a hope that subsequently proved vain—I wrote to the then Chief Secretary, stating these facts, and asking him to strike out from the sentence the words "hard labour," so as to enable Mr. Farrell to again enter public life in the county. To that letter I never had a reply, but I wrote again on the subject to Mr. James Bryce (afterwards British Ambassador at Washington, now Lord Bryce), when he was Chief Secretary, and received the following reply :

> "IRISH OFFICE,
> "OLD QUEEN STREET,
> "*December* 17, 1906.

"DEAR JUDGE CURRAN,

"The request in your letter of November 26th last, that the imposition of hard labour as part of the sentence inflicted on Mr. Farrell on October 24th should be obliterated, with a view to his again taking part in the local affairs of his county, was, I need hardly say, one to which I could not refuse my best consideration and my personal sympathy.

"I am very sorry, however, to have to inform you that, having taken legal advice on the point, I am told there is no legal power to obliterate part of a sentence, and so avoid the effect which we join in regretting.

> "Yours faithfully,
> "JAMES BRYCE.

"HIS HONOUR JUDGE CURRAN."

It is right to say that I wrote these letters without any suggestion or hint on the part of Mr. Farrell or of any of his friends, and I am quite sure that these pages contain the first intimation of the fact to him.

CHAPTER XXXII

WESTMEATH—LABOURERS ACTS—ENMITY BECOMES FRIENDSHIP

BOYCOTTING, cattle-driving, and malicious injuries were for many years very prevalent in the County Westmeath. I have not before me the figures showing the amount of compensation awarded by me for such injuries. I know it was considerable ; it included one-half of the sum of £1,370 awarded by me in the County Meath in Mr. William Dove's case.

What is known as a "Westmeath alibi" was always one which the Crown found it difficult to combat with success. A number of witnesses came forward who swore positively as to the presence of a prisoner at a particular time and place, which would render it impossible for him to have been present at the time and place of the alleged offence. No amount of cross-examination could break down their evidence, each corroborating his fellow-witness in the most minute particular. Their story was in one respect accurately true. They were all with the prisoners on a particular day, but not the day stated by the Crown witness. It is sad to relate that, when at the Bar, I was the means of acquitting many a prisoner with such a defence.

Cattle-driving continued very prevalent up to a late date in the County Westmeath. A gentleman of property in that county had his cattle driven off his lands on seven separate occasions. There had been previous drives, of which he took no notice, but he brought seven different applications for compensation, one for each drive. I gave him damages and costs in each case, the total amounting to a considerable sum.

Under the Act the Chairman has power to place the amount awarded on the entire county or upon any division of it. As I was aware that cattle-driving was carried on extensively throughout the county, in place of fixing the amount on the small area, part of which would, of course, be payable by the owner, who was a large ratepayer in the district, I put the sums awarded on the county at large, much to the indignation of my friend, Mr. E. Mason, solicitor for the County Council. At their next meeting the latter, who were very indignant, directed Mr. Mason to at once appeal, which was done. The case came on before Lord Justice Holmes, and that Judge was satisfied upon evidence that about that time cattle-driving was more or less prevalent in the entire county, and his lordship affirmed my decree, placing the several amounts and costs of appeal on the county at large.

I very seldom, except in extreme and very bad cases, imposed sentences of penal servitude. In the following case I considered it absolutely necessary for the public safety to pass such a sentence : Two men were tried by me at the Mullingar Quarter Sessions, charged with throwing stones from a railway bridge at a train as it passed underneath. It appeared from the evidence that there had been a strike among some of the employees of the Midland Great Western Railway in Athlone, in which the drivers and stokers refused to join. Stones were thrown at these men, with the result that one of them was seriously injured. The police were at first unable to detect any of the stone-throwers, as they varied the scene of their exploits from bridge to bridge; but at last two constables lay in wait and caught the two prisoners red-handed in the act of throwing stones at a train just passing underneath; others who were with them quickly disappeared. The two men were convicted.

I considered it a very serious case, the act endangering not only the lives of the men in charge of the engine, but also of the passengers in case the engine were deprived of the services of these men, and I sentenced both to three years' penal servitude. I was also influenced by the consideration that the sentence would act as a deterrent to others, and thus put a stop to the practice. It is needless to say that no more stone-throwing took place.

" Five years' penal servitude for stealing three-halfpence" was the newspaper heading of a case tried by me in one of the counties. The sub-editorial hand ignored the fact that the prisoner was proved to have broken into a dwelling-house, and took only three-halfpence because he could find no more; also, that the prisoner was a very old criminal, with a long record of previous convictions. The house broken into was that of a labourer. Such men are frequently absent from home working, and during their absence tramps and men of the prisoner's class were in the habit of breaking into their houses and taking any money or article they could lay their hands on. The sentence was also intended as a warning to parties similarly inclined.

The Labourers (Ireland) Acts were a great boon to the labouring classes. Under those Acts the District Council had the power to select sites of an acre or half an acre on the lands of adjoining proprietors, subject to the approval of the Local Government Inspector appointed to hear such cases. The landowners whose lands were taken had the right of appeal from the Inspector's decision to the Chairman of Quarter Sessions.

During my time I tried over 500 such appeals. In all the cases the labourers were examined before me, and I formed the opinion that they were a highly respectable body of men, well dressed, well educated, and a credit to their country. They appeared to me far superior in intelligence to many farmers or their sons. They had been miserably housed; their places of abode were as a rule a disgrace to civilization.

Lady Aberdeen well deserved the praise of all in calling attention to the necessity of taking precautions against the spread in Ireland of the dread disease of consumption. People were under the belief that that disease was one confined to the upper classes, who could alleviate it or retard its result by visiting foreign climates; but I was indeed horrified when, in hearing these appeals, I first became aware of the terrible ravages that fatal disease was, and had been, making among the poor and badly-housed labourers of Ireland.

Case after case came before me in which one or two, and sometimes three, members of the same family had been carried off by consumption. Some houses I found to be regular hotbeds of the disease, and I feel sure that by changing them from their miserable hovels into comfortable cottages with an acre of land, very much has been done to improve their position and to make it more endurable.

The entire power under the Acts was vested in the hands of the several District Councils, and these bodies, in the majority of cases, acted fairly and with justice to either side—landowner and tenant. Of course, human nature is human nature, and in such a number of cases you were bound to find some in which a district councillor kept a cottage off his own land or off that of a friendly neighbour, or put it on the land of an obnoxious one. I never allowed a cottage·to be put on the land of a boycotted person.

So, also, as a rule, the District Councils dealt fairly and leniently with their tenants, except where the latter disobeyed the orders of the local league in working for "obnoxious" persons. In such cases they showed no mercy, as the following examples will show: The tenant of a labourer's cottage named Colley, under the District Council of Mullingar, had been, it appeared, in the habit of working for a neighbouring lady who was boycotted. The members of the United Irish League of the district at once passed a resolution at one of their meetings condemning his action, calling the attention of the District Council to the fact, and demanding that he should be evicted from the cottage by that body. The Council, complying with the demand, took immediate steps to carry out their instructions, and served notice to quit on the labourer.

The case came before me at several Sessions, and eventually came on appeal before Mr. Justice Madden at the Mullingar Assizes, 1903. The learned Judge felt bound to grant a decree, but put a stay of six months on its execution.

Time after time I had endeavoured to induce the District Council to leave the man in his cottage, but without avail. I at length considered it my duty to bring the matter before the public. During the years when the County Westmeath was proclaimed under the Crimes Act, I was always of opinion, and so told the Grand Juries, that no law-abiding man needed to fear that Act, as it was only intended to affect law-breakers, or those who intended breaking the law. While the case of the Rural District Council against the labourer Colley was at hearing, I took occasion, in the month of October, 1902, to warn the Grand Jury against the danger of boycotting, which was then prevalent to a great extent in the county, though at the time it was very free from ordinary crime. I told them that no Judge on the Bench had had experience such as I had of the terrible results of boycotting; it very soon got beyond the control of those who started it, however innocently, and the pernicious system permeated every class of society; and I concluded by expressing a hope that the good sense of the people would put an end to its development in Westmeath.

After the Grand Jury had concluded their work, their foreman handed me down the following resolution: "That we, the Grand Jury of the County Westmeath, sitting at Mullingar Quarter Sessions, whilst congratulating the Mullingar District on its peaceful and crimeless condition, view with much apprehension the action of the Government in putting the Crimes Act in force in Westmeath, believing, as we do, that such action is unnecessary, and can result only in endangering the friendly relations existing between all classes in the county; and it is our deliberate opinion the Government would be well advised in removing the proclamation; and we wish that a copy of this resolution be forwarded to the Chief Secretary."

I told them that I should neither receive or forward their resolution, that comment on the action of the Government formed no part of their or my business, and that there were twenty-three of them on the jury, and let any one of them who felt coerced stand up. To this there was no reply; but, knowing that among its members there were at least three members of the Mullingar Rural District Council—a body which had been hounding down the unfortunate labourer Colley, simply because he had exercised his lawful right to work for a boycotted lady—I tore up in their presence their resolution, saying I treated it as so much waste paper.

Some five years later, in the year 1908, Mr. Nicholas J. Downes, as solicitor for the Mullingar Rural District Council, appeared before me in three ejectment processes at the suit of that Council, seeking to evict three labourers named respectively

Colman, Dack, and Donnelly. The three men had for several years been tenants of the Council for labourers' cottages. During their tenancy their employer, Mr. Harry Bond, of Fairy Hill, landed proprietor and agent, was very wickedly boycotted. I have already referred to his case.

The Council at one of their meetings passed a resolution calling upon the three defendants to leave Mr. Bond's employment, and, on their refusal to do so, served them with notice to quit, and I had to try the ejectments founded on them. I felt bound by the decree of Mr. Justice Madden in the case of Colley, and pronounced a decree, and, also acting on that Judge's view, put a lengthened stay on it by increasing the stay of six months imposed by him to eleven months, stating that I did so in order to show my disapproval and condemnation of the Council's action in using the power and authority vested in them by law for the benefit of the labouring class for political purposes. The Judge of Assize, in affirming my decree, removed the stay. I was glad it was his act, not mine.

On another occasion the Grand Jury passed a resolution refusing coal to the court-house or my chamber, and but for the kindness of the Sheriff, who supplied all the fuel required, I should indeed have had a very cold sitting. However, they did not try it a second time, as at a subsequent Sessions I covered with ridicule their puny efforts in the obstruction of justice, describing their action as that of so many " play-boys."

One of the many incidents of our proximity to England is the fact that no local body in Ireland can have an Act of Parliament passed, or obtain its benefits, unless they have their case examined into and tried by the committee of the House—sitting, of course, in London ; with the necessary result that all the witnesses have to be taken to that city.

The case of the Mullingar waterworks was, from this point of view, a peculiarly hard one to rate-payers of the district. The Council had settled upon a suitable place from which to take a water-supply, and duly obtained from Parliament the right to construct the works, but a certain limit of time was fixed for carrying out the undertaking. Immediately after they had obtained the Act the Most Rev. Dr. Nulty, Bishop of the diocese—who considered himself a bit of an engineer—wrote to the Council, stating that it would be an unnecessary expense to construct a reservoir under their Act, as he could supply them with a sufficiency of water from a tank on the top of a building on his grounds.

A long and bitter controversy followed in the Council as to the acceptance of his lordship's offer. Opinion was much divided, but eventually Dr. Nulty's offer was accepted by a majority. One of the principal opponents to the Bishop's offer was Mr. Hayden, M.P. for Roscommon.

18

Controversy continued between the supporters of Dr. Nulty's offer and Mr. Hayden, who was owner of a local newspaper. In the course of it Mr. Hayden was denounced from the altar, and people were forbidden to read or buy his paper.

I sometimes had a friendly chat with that gentleman on my way home from Sessions, when he also would be on his way to Dublin. I met him on the evening of the day he had been denounced. A lady member of his family had heard the fact when attending Mass. Mr. Hayden felt, as might be expected, very irate, aggrieved, and sore; but his revenge came very soon. The Inspector from the Local Government Board, after inspection, reported that though Dr. Nulty's supply of water was sufficient for the military barracks, which his lordship was at the time supplying, it would be quite insufficient to supply both the barracks and the town of Mullingar. For this reason the contract of the Council with Dr. Nulty fell through, and the former had to fall back on their original resolution—to procure their own supply. On consideration of the matter it was found that the time limit mentioned in the Act had expired, and for this reason they were driven to the necessity of having a new Act and Order passed, after having uselessly expended, as I understood, over £500 on the first. Mullingar, however, has now a very plentiful supply from Lough Owel, which is only a short distance from the town.

Mr. Farrell, M.P., during all these years used very strong language against me in the columns of his journal, the *Longford Leader*. Having regard to the fact that I had felt myself coerced to affirm against him a sentence of two months' imprisonment under the Crimes Act, I always considered he had some ground for resentment against me. Accordingly, during the Sessions before I resigned, hearing that he was very ill, I went to see him. He was in bed, but seemed very pleased to see me, and we had a very warm shake hands. "No more, Judge, no more," were the words he used. I replied that "I hoped there was many a kick left in him yet," and then enmity ceased, and a friendship, which I hope will be lasting, took its place. I little thought how soon that kick was to come. Here it is :

"MARKET SQUARE,
      "LONGFORD,
            "*January* 3, 1914.

"JUDGE ADYE CURRAN, K.C.,
      "DUBLIN.

"DEAR JUDGE CURRAN,

"I am joined by my wife and son Gerald, and indeed all my children, in expressing to you our great regret to learn from this evening's paper of your resignation as County Court Judge of Longford, with which you have been so long connected. Notwithstanding our many political fights, I always liked your fatherly, humane style of dealing with the cases before you. I hope and trust you will have a long old age before being called to a better life.

" With every good New Year's wish and deep regret,

"I am, sincerely yours,

"J. P. FARRELL."

I received many letters of regret, praise, and commendation on my retirement in the month of January, 1914, but not one of them did I value more than the above letter from the quondam opponent of my action during twenty-seven years in the County Longford, showing that however he may have disapproved of my conduct in endeavouring to protect the victims of boycotting, he was, at all events, ready to give me credit for good intentions.

In the hope that matters are now quieting down, and that bygones may be bygones, I have said little here as to the acts of boycotting denounced by me from time to time, and I conclude by expressing the earnest wish that these terrible times for the unfortunate victims of this nefarious system may never be repeated in Irish history.

CHAPTER XXXIII

RANDOM MEMORIES—"JUDGES" AND "CHAIRMEN"

THE courts in the Midland Counties were as full of interest as those in Kerry. A prisoner came before me in one of the Midland Counties, charged with horse-stealing. The case against him was very clearly proved, but he very evidently had some friends on the jury, and the result was an acquittal. As a rule, jurors, nearly all of them, are—from selfish motives—very anxious to convict parties charged with horse or cattle stealing, and I suspected that strong pressure must have been brought to bear in the case.

In reading out a long list of convictions for horse-stealing against the prisoner, I advised him, if he still intended to carry on his evil practices in the county, he might for choice look up the horses of the twelve gentlemen in the jury-box, as they seemed to think there was no harm in horse-stealing. Having regard to the prisoner's previous record, and my advice to him, I am quite sure I made them feel somewhat repentant and nervous.

Once when I was trying a man for assault in Killarney, during the examination of the chief witness as to the facts of the assault, we were startled by one of the jurors calling out suddenly : "You are a liar!" To my indignant query as to the meaning of such an interruption, he replied : "Ah, your Honour, was I not looking at it myself?" As I quite agreed with him as to the want of veracity on the part of the witness, I did no more than mildly reprimand him for his Celtic impulsiveness. I then let the case go to them, and, of course, an acquittal was the result.

In an equity suit by a mortgagee, before me in one of the Midland Counties, I had to sell the mortgaged lands. The mortgagor refused to execute the conveyance when presented to him for signature. In the court, contrary to the advice of his solicitor, he positively refused to sign the deed, and said he did not care what I did, as he had nothing to lose, his passage to America having been paid. Whenever possible, I always avoided directing my Registrar to execute deeds, and told the man I should have to commit him unless he obeyed the order of Court. He again refused, flourishing what he said was his ticket. I said I did not believe him. "See for yourself," he replied, handing me up what I saw was really a passage ticket to America. I handed it down to the Clerk of the Crown and Peace, directing him not to return it until the deed had been executed. After some bluster and loud talk, the man obeyed my order, and he was given back his ticket.

I always mistrusted witnesses who took care to inform me, in the course of their evidence, that at the time they were just going to or coming from the church. In one case a witness was being examined before me. I was rather inclined to think that he was not telling the truth. Suddenly, in the middle of a sentence, he bowed his head and kept it so for two or three minutes. All in court thought he was ill, and some concern in his regard was expressed when he looked up; I asked him what was the matter. To the amusement and laughter of all in court, he informed me he had been saying the Angelus. I no longer had any doubt as to his want of veracity, and so I told him.

Some time afterwards, when I was trying a prisoner in the county town, I had again before me a pious witness. I was proceeding to tell the jury of my experience as above stated, when I perceived some show of merriment among the solicitors, and a stage whisper came up to me, " Take care, he is on the jury." I may mention, I did not conclude the story.

For some years after the passing of the Licensing Acts (Ireland) the Crown claimed the right to appeal in cases where magistrates refused to convict in charges brought before them against publicans and others for breaches of the provisions of those Acts.

The practice continued for several years, until owing to an English decision its legality became doubtful.

Such a case came before me in a Midland town, where a publican had been charged with having sold drink during prohibited hours to a number of men whom the police found on his premises. The defendant and each of the men swore that the latter only asked for tobacco, which was supplied to them, some taking an ounce, others half an ounce. The two amounts struck me as peculiar, and I accordingly recalled one of the men, who, however willing to prevaricate, I thought would hesitate before committing perjury, and I finally elicited from him the fact that one ounce of tobacco meant a glass of whisky, and half an ounce half a glass, and that in paying for the ounce of tobacco, which happened to be the price of a glass of whisky, both whisky and tobacco were given to him, and after drinking the whisky he handed back to the publican the tobacco, which then did duty for the next applicant. As the men swallowed the whisky, so did the magistrates swallow their story, and dismissed the case—an order which I felt no difficulty in reversing.

Whenever in the framing of an Act of Parliament it became necessary to appoint new duties to be performed, those duties were, whenever possible, assigned to the unfortunate County Court Judge, without, of course, any increase in his salary, and so, as time went on, the Judge's duties became very mixed and onorous.

The jurisdiction of the Irish County Court Judges, including that of Chairman of Quarter Sessions, is of a very varied description. Their jurisdiction in Crown cases is practically unlimited except to a very small extent. They try appeals from magistrates, involving the knowledge of the many matters which can be brought before that tribunal.

The rent limit in ejectment is £100, in ordinary cases £50. They were sole Judges in hearing appeals under the Crimes Act. They are now sole Judges in hearing cases under the Master and Servants Act and Workmen's Compensation Acts, and also for hearing applications for compensation for malicious injuries. They have also to deal with the Licensing Law, and applications for new licences and transfers under it; also Valuation and Income Tax appeals, and they have an extensive though limited jurisdiction in nearly all civil cases. They have all the power of the Court of Chancery in all equity cases where the valuation of the land does not exceed £30, or the amount involved does not exceed £500. They have a like jurisdiction in Probate and Lunacy cases. I have already referred to the various duties imposed on them under the Land Law (Ireland) Acts, to which I may add the hearing of applications under the Town Tenants (Ireland) Acts.

I had a very considerable amount of trouble in

dealing with the estates of minors. Many of these minors, of course, became of age during my time, and I always did my best to safeguard their interests even after they had left my court.

In one of my counties I had a very sad case. It was an equity suit by a wife against her husband and members of his family, to enforce specific performance of a marriage settlement. I pronounced a decree in favour of the wife, giving her the farm, which had been the subject-matter of the suit. Very shortly afterwards the wife was murdered by her husband, and the husband was subsequently convicted of her murder and executed. They left two little children, and these, thanks to the charity of a friend, have since been housed and cared for. I made them wards of Court. They had some little property, which I have safeguarded carefully for them, and they are now under the care of my successor.

My principal difficulty arose when a widow with young children married a second time. If the children happened to be entitled to property which they had derived from their father, I made them wards of Court, and then it became a constant struggle on the part of the mother and stepfather to get every shilling of the children's money under every imaginable pretext. These pretexts, I need not say, I rigorously sifted.

Owing to the multitudinous duties thrown on the Irish County Court Judges, I often compared the court to what is known in the country as a "strong shop," where every conceivable commodity is sold. At the various counters you find jewellery, bacon, stationery, groceries, hardware, ironmongery, furniture, drink for sale on and off the premises, and a vast miscellany, including agricultural implements.

In addition, the Irish County Court Judges have, in whole or in part, to revise the Parliamentary Roll, a duty which their English brethren are not called upon to perform.

No one can sit upon the Bench for as many years as I have without having some experience of red-tapeism. One example, in which the official concerned endeavoured to extricate himself at his own expense, I give here: In sending in my expense docket to the Treasury, I on one occasion charged the sum of 4s. 11d. as the fare from Mullingar to Longford. Shortly afterwards I received a letter from a friend in the office to the effect that the Treasury clerks in London had stopped the sum of 2d. from my account, as the fare was 4s. 9d., and not 4s. 11d., as charged by me.

When next in Mullingar, I inquired the price of the ticket, and I found I was right, and I got a receipt for the 4s. 11d. The clerks on the other side had deducted the full fare from Dublin to Mullingar from that from Dublin to Longford, which amounted to 4s. 9d., but did not take into account the fact that a short fare between two intermediate stations might be greater in proportion.

I immediately wrote to my friend at the Castle, enclosing the receipt, and demanding back my twopence. He replied, admitting the error, but rather than enter into a lengthy correspondence with the Treasury clerks in London, offered to pay the amount out of his own pocket. In answer, I wrote refusing to take the twopence from him, and insisted that it should be refunded by the Treasury in London, who had made the mistake.

My friend's reply, in not very complimentary language, I do not repeat, but it plainly intimated that he had no notion of asking the London folk to return the money, and so I have been obliged to do without the twopence to this day.

When I was first appointed County Court Judge, I found it was the custom that the last appointed Judge should act as secretary to the body. I came to the conclusion that this plan did not work in a satisfactory manner. There was no continuity in our action, as no secretary occupied the position for any length of time, and for this reason I suggested that I should act until I resigned, or, as they kindly put it, was " dismissed." I accordingly held the lucrative post for several years, until I handed it over to the late Judge Anderson.

During my term of office I successfully carried through all its stages a *Gazette* order giving the Irish County Court Judges the same rank and title as that enjoyed by our English brethren, and declaring them entitled to the prefix and appella-

tion of " Judge " instead of " County Court Judge."
Some of the older members were rather opposed to
my action, on the ground that our position as
" Chairman of Quarter Sessions," with almost unlimited criminal jurisdiction, placed us above the
English Judges of the County Court, these Judges
having no such jurisdiction.

It is well to add that the various sections in Acts
of Parliament withdrawing certain offences from
Quarter Sessions have never been held to apply to
Ireland. The Chairman in England is generally
some local non-legal magnate, while those in Ireland
must be barristers of at least ten years' standing.
I have during my experience of over thirty years
tried many cases outside the jurisdiction of English
chairmen.

Commencing as its secretary in the year 1883,
I became senior member and chairman after the
death of Sir Francis W. Brady, and so continued
till I retired on January 3, 1914.

CHAPTER XXXIV

FAREWELL

My relations with the Clerks of the Crown and Peace in the several counties over which I presided as Chairman have invariably been of the most friendly nature. I include among them the late Mr. Stephen Huggard, who, during my five years in Kerry, filled that important position. During that period I always experienced the greatest hospitality from both himself and the members of his family. I can say the same of the present holder of the office, Mr. Francis Creagh Downing, and his family.

Mr. James P. Fagan, the present Clerk of the Crown and Peace for the King's County, was appointed to his position in the end of 1883, a very short time after my own appointment, and during the thirty years we have worked together in the administration of justice, not a word ever passed between us which was not of the most friendly nature. Indeed, he frequently took upon himself work which, properly speaking, belonged to the Judge. On my retirement I parted from many old and sincere friends, but I felt no parting more acutely than that with James P. Fagan.

Mr. John Forbes O'Farrell practised before me as a solicitor for many years before he was appointed Clerk of the Crown and Peace for Longford, and as he was personally acquainted with many of those who came before me from his part of the county, his advice was always most valuable and trustworthy. I found him a most efficient officer and a great favourite all round. I had known his father before him, a solicitor of the old school, who sometimes honoured me with a brief.

I resigned my late position some two days before the appointment of Mr. Patrick Robert Kelly as Clerk of the Crown and Peace for the County Westmeath; nevertheless, Mr. Kelly claimed his right to join the other Clerks of the Crown and Peace in the beautiful presentation made to me by them, hereafter mentioned.

Mr. Kelly, however, had practised before me in the county as a solicitor, and for some years past filled the responsible position of Crown Solicitor, and I had every opportunity of judging of his great ability and efficiency. He succeeded as Clerk of the Crown and Peace that grand old man, William Mooney, whom I remembered from the time I went on circuit as a young barrister. In those old days I was always sure of an appeal brief from him. In court for many years he was ably represented by Mr. F. Davis.

When I returned from Kerry to the County Meath towards the close of the year 1891, I found there installed in the position of Clerk of the Crown and Peace a gentleman who was a stranger to me—Mr. George Knight. He gave me a most kind and friendly greeting. I took a fancy to him from the first, and from that day we have continued close and intimate friends. All through these long years, both socially and officially, I have received from him at all times the greatest courtesy and help. No work was too heavy for him, provided he considered he thereby lessened mine. The severance of my official connection with the dearest of friends was a very severe wrench, notwithstanding their generous attempts to soften that wrench.

On April 29 last I was presented by the Clerks of the Crown and Peace for the counties of Westmeath, Meath, King's County and Longford, with a beautiful specimen of art, a large and splendid silver representation of the old Ardagh Chalice. It bore the following inscription :

> "To his Honour Judge Adye Curran, K.C., from his friends the Clerks of the Crown and Peace for the Counties of King's, Meath, Longford, and Westmeath. In affectionate remembrance of cordial relationship. 29th of April, 1914."

With the exception of some three or four old

friends who greeted me on my arrival in 1883—
notably Mr. John Wilson of Longford, Mr. Patrick
J. Nooney, Mr. Nicholas J. J. Downes, and Mr.
William P. Kelly of Westmeath—all my practitioners commenced their professional lives before
me.

I was most fortunate in my four Crown Solicitors.
All of them are men of great ability, and each
started his career before me. There could be no
more able Crown Solicitor or advocate than Mr.
Thomas W. Delany, Crown Solicitor for Longford.
Commencing, as I have said, before me, he has
gradually attained the highest point in his profession. What I have said of Mr. Delany I can
also repeat as to Mr. Richard J. Barry in the
King's County, and Mr. P. R. Kelly in Westmeath.
I had only known Mr. John G. Fottrell as a practitioner before me for some few years, but I anticipate
the interests of the Crown will be well guarded by
him. I may add that I have known him from his
childhood.

I must also add a few words of regret on
parting from my old and sincere friend, Mr.
James V. Dunn, who for the past thirty years has
been my Registrar. He succeeded in that post
another dear friend, Mr. John C. Ennis, who had
held it for a short time. Mr. Dunn was a most
efficient officer. During those many years as Judge
and Registrar, or as travelling companions, a cross
word never passed the lips of either of us, and I

19

parted from Mr. Dunn, both as officer and friend, with a saddened heart.

Remembering my own diffidence, and the struggle I had at the beginning of my professional career, I determined to assist in every way young practitioners coming before me for the first time. I continued doing this until such time as they were able to "paddle their own canoe," with the result that much mutual affectionate regard sprang up, and continued during the many years of professional association.

On the same 29th of April, 1914, nearly every one of the solicitors, over fifty in number, came before me in the Incorporated Law Society's room, kindly lent for the occasion, when Master Denning, formerly one of my practitioners, and now acting as spokesman, on their behalf presented me with a solid silver tea and coffee service, bearing the following inscription :

> "Presented to John Adye Curran, Esq., K.C., by the solicitors of the Counties of Meath, Westmeath, King's County, and Longford, as a token of esteem, on his resignation of the position of County Court Judge. January, 1914."

At the same time I was presented by them with an address in the following words :

> "To JOHN ADYE CURRAN, ESQ., K.C.
>
> "We the undersigned solicitors practising in the County Courts of Meath, Westmeath,

King's County, and Longford, beg your acceptance on your retirement from the position of County Court Judge, of a slight token of the esteem and respect which we feel for you and Mrs. Curran.

"During an intercourse of many years, we have learned to appreciate your sterling worth and sincerity of purpose, and we hope that our little offering may be a daily reminder to you, in your well earned leisure, of the kindly relations that existed between you and us, and of our good wishes which you carry with you."

It was signed by the following gentlemen, grouped according to counties:

County Meath:

A. V. Montgomery, John George Fottrell, C.S., Ambrose Steen, R. Norman Potterton, Francis C. O'Reilly, Patrick J. Tallon, James M. J. Lynch, William H. Spence, Daniel J. Reilly, James J. Magee, Charles Murphy, F. G. McKeever, Thomas Tiernan, Messrs. Brown and McCann, William L. B. Cochrane, William D. Sullivan, T. C. Ross.

King's County:

Messrs. Hoey and Denning, Richard F. Barry, C.S., Messrs. A. and L. Goodbody, Thomas Conway, James Rogers, Thomas O'Kearney, White, Thomas Mitchel, James Mitchel, J. J. Kennedy, M. J. O'Meara, J. F. Power

C. J. Spain, William Dwyer, A. C. Houlahan.

County Westmeath :

Nicholas J. Downes, Patrick J. Nooney, John J. Macken, Arthur G. Riggs, Edwin E. Mason, E. A. Shaw, Joseph Shaw, Thomas J. Dowdal, C.S., P. V. C. Murtagh, Charles E. Fair, Robert Elder, Edmond Mooney, Wm. P. Kelly.

County Longford :

Thomas W. Delaney, C.S., John Wilson Michael M. Kenny, C. J. P. Farrell, John J. Ham, F. G. Magan, John E. Wallace, P. J. Mallon, George F. Montgomery.

I am aware that many members of my own profession who had practised before me were anxious to join in the presentation, but were precluded from doing so owing to the wish of the solicitors to confine it to their own body. However, two young friends, barristers, both of whom commenced their career before me about ten years before I resigned, presented me shortly after that event with a large silver cigar and cigarette box, inside which is the following inscription :

HIS HONOUR JUDGE CURRAN.

FROM

A. E. W. AND E. S. M.

I have already referred to one of the two, Mr. Edward S. Murphy. The other is Mr. Albert Edward Wood, whom I am also glad to see coming to the front rank in his profession.

As a book dealing with a man's own career and experiences can hardly be deemed complete without a reference to the members of his family, a short digression into matters appertaining to my domestic circle will be pardoned.

I was married in the month of April, 1864, to my dear wife, Rose Mary, eldest daughter of the late Denis B. Kelly, J.P., whose father came originally from a place called Cloncanon, in the County Galway, and afterwards settled in Athlone, County Roscommon.

After a long and very happy married life, we celebrated our Golden Jubilee just a year ago. I am glad to be able to say that now as I write, in the autumn of 1915, we two have still good reason to thank God for the blessing of health liberally vouchsafed to us.

We have had four children, three girls and one boy; one girl died in infancy; our only boy, Jack, died many years ago, aged about sixteen. Of my two surviving daughters, the elder, Susie, was married to Daniel Mahony, the able and efficient Dublin Police Magistrate, whose good work, so well known to the citizens of Dublin, has, to our great sorrow, been recently closed by his death. The younger, Frances, remains with us, the help and companion of her mother and myself.

We three have travelled much together, both at home and abroad. In my early days my favourite trip consisted of the long sea trip to London and back or ten days in Scotland. In later times we were enabled to extend our travels. For several years we spent the spring in Rome, and visited many other countries. My wife and daughter spent two winters in the Canary Islands, in the vain hope of improving the health of our boy, and in the interval of my sittings at Sessions I used to fit in a trip to see them.

The last milestone of memory is almost reached, and I must bring these Reminiscences, the plain tale of a plain, blunt man, to a conclusion. They were written to beguile the weary hours of idleness which followed upon a full half-century of busy, and, alas! too swiftly fleeting, years. They are published, as I pointed out at the beginning, to tell the story of the Invincible conspiracy and its true inwardness. But I give them into your hands and to the world with yet another object.

They will serve to keep green the memory of many dear friends who have gone before, and they will say farewell—for indeed it seems to be the final parting—to those of later years who still remain.

No note or jotting of the moment, nor yet a diary of the passing show of life, has come to my aid, and save for some kindly help in the compilation, which was given to me by two or three friends, including Joseph B. Lee, Barrister-at-Law, now a Lieutenant in the Royal Munster Fusiliers, my book is of my own making, and is the product of a happily retentive mind.

Amongst the many mercies which Providence has bestowed on me, none has been greater than the partial restoration of my eyesight, which I nearly lost some years ago, and I have thus been enabled to write these Reminiscences with my own hand.

My story, in the main, has been concerned with the sordid and unhappy struggles of my strife-riven but dearly beloved country. As these closing lines are written while the shadow of war has fallen across the threshold of the Empire which owes not a little of its grandeur and power to those great Irishmen who helped in part to fashion it, and who still guard its destinies on sea and land, I may hope that the stress of the conflict may anneal for ever the divisions of my countrymen, and that the new generation may know our Ireland governed by principles of justice and right.

Since finishing these lines I have learned with the deepest regret of the death of two young members of the Irish Bar, who commenced their professional career before me. Relinquishing their chances of success at the Bar, they placed their services during the present war at the command of their King and country.

One, Lieutenant Joseph B. Lee, 6th Royal Munster Fusiliers, whom I have mentioned as giving me such assistance in the compilation of these Memoirs, was a splendid type of officer and man, being over six feet high, and a great personal friend. He was, I grieve to say, killed in action at the Dardanelles on the 7th of the present August.

The other, Lieutenant Gerald Plunkett, son of a near neighbour, joined the Navy, and was also killed in action some short time before, at the Dardanelles.

INDEX

BILLING AND SONS, LTD., PRINTERS, GUILDFORD, ENGLAND

Lightning Source UK Ltd.
Milton Keynes UK
UKHW032127280322
400748UK00004B/484